BIBLICAL
imagination
SERIES

JOHN
The Gospel of Wisdom

MICHAEL CARD

IVP Books

An imprint of InterVarsity Press
Downers Grove, Illinois

InterVarsity Press
P.O. Box 1400, Downers Grove, IL 60515-1426
World Wide Web: www.ivpress.com
Email: email@ivpress.com

InterVarsity Press® is the book-publishing division of InterVarsity Christian Fellowship/USA®, a movement of students and faculty active on campus at hundreds of universities, colleges and schools of nursing in the United States of America, and a member movement of the International Fellowship of Evangelical Students. For information about local and regional activities, write Public Relations Dept., InterVarsity Christian Fellowship/USA, 6400 Schroeder Rd., P.O. Box 7895, Madison, WI 53707-7895, or visit the IVCF website at www.intervarsity.org.

Design: Cindy Kiple
Image: The Healing of the Blind Man, "The Four Gospels" at Mount Athos Monastery, Iberon, Greece, Erich Lessing/ Art Resource, NY

ISBN 978-0-8308-4413-5 (print)
ISBN 978-0-8308-7970-0 (digital)

Printed in the United States of America ∞

As a member of the Green Press Initiative, InterVarsity Press is committed to protecting the environment and to the responsible use of natural resources. To learn more, visit greenpressinitiative.org.

Library of Congress Cataloging-in-Publication Data

Card, Michael, 1957-
  John : the gospel of wisdom / Michael Card.
    pages cm.—(Biblical imagination series)
  Includes bibliographical references.
  ISBN 978-0-8308-4413-5 (pbk. : alk. paper)
  1. Bible. John—Commentaries. I. Title.
  BS2615.53.C37 2014
  226.5'077—dc23

                                                              2014013200

P 20 19 18 17 16 15 14 13 12 11 10 9

Y 31 30 29 28 27 26 25 24 23 22 21

This book is dedicated with deep respect to Anthony Pickett,
whose friendship, concern for the community and love
for the Gospel of John has been a constant
encouragement for so many years.

CONTENTS

THE BIBLICAL IMAGINATION

*"On the last and greatest day of the feast, Jesus stood
and said in a loud voice, "If anyone is thirsty,
let him come to me and drink . . ."*

JOHN 7:37 NIV

*A*t first it seems simple enough. Jesus is in Jerusalem for some sort of feast and is announcing to the crowd that if they come to him, he will somehow satisfy their thirst. A bit vague . . . It is the stuff of a nice devotional. That is how I read John 7:37 specifically and the Bible in general before someone helped me to learn to engage and really listen. If any single verse is responsible for opening the door of my imagination to engage with the Scripture, it is this verse.

On a hot summer morning on the third floor of Cherry Hall at Western Kentucky University, William Lane opened that door by asking a few simple questions.

"What feast?" he asked.

None of us knew.

"Look back at verse 2," he said.

Verse 2 of chapter 7 says the feast was Tabernacles, also known as Succoth, or sometimes Booths.

"Does anyone know what occurs on the last day of the Feast of Tabernacles?"

Another long uncomfortable silence . . .

With an intensity we were slowly becoming accustomed to, Dr. Lane began to quote (from memory) an obscure passage from the Mishnah, the collected teachings of the rabbis between 200 B.C. to A.D. 200. From a section called Sukkah (4:1, 9-10) he explained that on the last and greatest day of the Feast of Tabernacles the high priest would lead a procession to the pool of Siloam. Before the congregation he would dip a pitcher into the pool. The crowd would return to the temple, chanting psalms like 118:25, "Save now, we beseech thee, O Jehovah" (ASV). When the crowd arrived again at the temple, the high priest would raise the pitcher high and pour its contents on the ground. This commemorated Moses striking the rock in the wilderness and the provision of water for the people of God. At this moment he would proclaim, "With joy you will draw water from the wells of salvation," a passage from the prophet Isaiah (12:3 ESV).

"Now take that information and return to the passage," Bill said.

It is difficult to find the words to describe the difference reading John 7:37 with that background. This was the first time I had ever read the Bible with an *informed* imagination. The words on the page that a moment ago were a dry devotion became a motion picture in full color. I put two and two together and saw Jesus standing in the midst of that crowd, perhaps somewhere in the back. As the words of the high priest died out, a voice, a shouting voice, from the back of the crowd cries out, "If anyone is thirsty, he should come to Me and drink."

The thought of it still takes my breath away over thirty years later. If that is what engaging with the Scripture is like, I decided then and there that I would give the rest of my life to doing just that, delving deeper into the Bible to find the backgrounds that make the stories come to life.

"We must engage the Scripture at the level of the informed imagination," Bill said too many times to count. And many of the elements of that approach are evident in this story. First, we stopped and asked a few simple questions of the text, simple, yet better questions than we had thought to ask. John says it was the last day of the feast, trusting that we have been listening, assuming that we have read large blocks of his Gospel and not simply one or two verses. Thirty-five verses earlier he told us it was Tabernacles. He assumes we were listening. But I had not been paying attention.

Next we did our homework, or Bill did our homework for us. Again it led to one of those better questions, "What happens on the last and greatest day of the Feast of Tabernacles?"

It is always the informed imagination. We must become committed to doing the work, to finding the best sources, beginning with the primary sources, the earliest writings: Mishnah, Talmud, Josephus, Pliny, Suetonius and Tacitus. These ancient sources do not exist only for the scholars. They are all readily available, now more than ever with electronic books. (Many of them are free!) When we returned to the text with an informed imagination we were ready to engage, and what happened changed our lives, changed everything. The facts in the mind combined with the devotion of the heart, across that bridge of the imagination, all under the guidance and control of the Spirit and the Word came to life. You and I are there with the crowd in the cool fall air. (Tabernacles is a fall festival celebrating the harvest.) Our legs are sore since we've just climbed the steep hill from the pool of Siloam, at the bottom of the ridge, to the temple, which dominates the top of the hill. At the moment we are thirsty, thirsty and out of breath. We hear an ordinary voice shouting those luminous words from the back of the mob. How do we respond? To find him, to see his face, to fall down confessing our thirst, our sin, our need, our hunger for him. Once you experience this sort of engagement with Scripture, nothing will ever be the same.

WHO IS JOHN?

John is ink-fingered and aged. He is a living legend near the end of life, far past where the end is supposed to be. He is the last of the Twelve. Paul considered him one of the pillars (Gal 2:9). His brother, James, the first of the disciples to die, was martyred almost sixty years ago (A.D. 44). John cared for Jesus' mother till the day she died. Though death seems to be all around him now, unsettlingly close, he is still very much alive and quietly obsessed with a single question, What is love? It is the concern that ties his first and longest letter together.

That we possess three of his letters seems almost a miracle. They are a precious glimpse into his pastor's heart. Over and over again he tenderly addresses his readers as "dear children" and "dear friends." In his last two frustratingly short letters he closes by saying that he would write more, but longs to see them face-to-face. The teenage eyewitness and follower has developed a pastor's heart, and like most pastors' hearts, it is broken. Sometimes I imagine him writing those words to me, "Michael, I would write more, but I long to see you face-to-face."

His voice is wonderfully present in the letters, so evident and clear and strong you can almost hear its tone. His amazement still echoes: what "we have heard . . . seen with our eyes . . . have touched with our hands!" (1 Jn 1:1). Any translation that does not insert an exclamation mark after that statement has missed the point entirely. They are the amazed words of a once angry young man. Decades later, having preached and taught the life of Jesus to his "children" and "friends," he has developed what theologians refer to as a "high Christology." For John, Jesus is light and life, and the One through whom God created the universe. Yet he had heard Jesus' voice, had seen his luminous face, had even touched his hand.

John was the junior partner in a successful fishing business with his father Zebedee, his brother James, and his friends Andrew and Simon, the sons of Jonah. The indications of their success were the fact that they had hired servants (Mk 1:20) and that John's mother, Salome, was able to help support the ministry of Jesus out of her finances (Mk 15:41). One of the questions raised by scholars in the past has been how could John possess such intimate knowledge and interest in the city of Jerusalem when he was clearly from Galilee? He knows the name of the high priest's servant as well as the slave girl who minds the gate at the house of Annas. She seems to know him personally (Jn 18:15-16). Perhaps the success of his father's fishing business explains how a boy from the north of Galilee would know the big city of Jerusalem so well. Perhaps he had sold fish there.

I find it fascinating that two of the Gospels were written by men whose mothers were among the first followers of Jesus. There is Mark, whose mother, Mary, opened her home to the church in Jerusalem (Acts 12:12). The other is John. Salome, his mother, was one of the women who followed Jesus during his first mission (Mt 27:56; Mk 15:40-41). She was at the cross (Mk 15:40) standing beside her son. She was present at the tomb on resurrection morning (Mk 16:1-2). She has been criticized for making what seems an overly ambitious request of Jesus, to allow her two sons to sit on either side of him in the kingdom (Mt 20:20-28). Given the fact that Jesus had just promised his disciples twelve thrones, it is not completely unreasonable that she wanted to adjust the seating arrangement in their favor.

Perhaps most remarkable, we can infer from John 19:25 and Mark 15:40 that Salome may have been the sister of Mary, the mother of Jesus. This would mean Jesus and John would have been cousins. If this is true it would help explain Jesus' remarkable request that John care for his mother, a request he made from the cross (Jn 19:26-27). And care for her he did, according to Eusebius, taking Mary with him to Ephesus, where he was present with her when she died.[1]

The final piece of the puzzle of John's life is the matter of his great age, so great in fact that it gave birth to a rumor that he would not die till Jesus returned (Jn 21:23). A preliminary answer is provided by some speculative math. Clement of Alexandria says John lived until the reign of Trajan.[2] This would put his death around A.D. 98. Tradition says he was roughly one hundred years old. While remarkable, it was not unheard of for people to live this long in the first century. Ovid's father lived to be ninety. Though we do not know his precise age, Simeon lived to an old age. The great Hillel, the foremost teacher in Israel just before the time of Jesus, lived to be 110.[3] At a time when infant mortality was high and the average age of death was well before fifty, admittedly one hundred is near miraculous. Clearly the rumor which John 21:23 addresses was a result of John's remarkable age.

An impetuous young eyewitness who has matured through ministry and persecution into a gentle, brokenhearted pastor, John has taught the life of Jesus over and over to the point that his teaching has come together in themes and has developed into his high Christology. As a preacher he has had vast experience in recapturing the imaginations of his listeners, a style reminiscent in many ways of Jesus.

LEARNING TO LISTEN TO JOHN

One of the keys to engaging with the text at the level of the informed imagination is to take the facts and learn to ask what they mean. If these facts about who John was are true and the speculations are even reasonably sound, what would we expect from such a person? It is not enough to collect facts like a stamp collector collects stamps. If we are to engage with our imaginations, we must to learn to discover what the facts mean.

If John was indeed an eyewitness, what might we expect from his account of the life of Jesus? Whenever eyewitnesses give their accounts of incidents, they offer details that only someone who was physically present would know. This is exactly what we find in John's Gospel. He gives to us the time of day incidents occur (Jn 1:39; 4:6; 19:14). He whispers asides about the motivations of the characters in his stories (Jn 2:24; 7:7). He provides distances that only an eyewitness would have known (Jn 6:19; 21:8). Be on the lookout as we work through the Gospel of John for these kinds of eyewitness details.

If John was indeed a pastor, as the later traditions and his three letters suggest, what might we expect from a Gospel written by a pastor? Certainly we would expect to find sermons, which is exactly what we find in John's Gospel. The prologue (Jn 1:1-14) is one of the greatest sermons ever written. Later in the Gospel, John will provide what I refer to as "sermonic conclusions." In these he will reach back into proceeding material and tie his various themes together. Frequently these smaller sermonic blocks will contain a single verse statement of the plan of salvation. The sermons are often mistakenly attributed to Jesus (Jn 1:1-5, 10-14, 16-18; 3:13-21, 31-36; 20:30-31).

The location of the writing of a New Testament document is always a major consideration in terms of understanding its content. The Gospel of Mark was written in Rome just after the great fire of A.D. 64. This fact provides a helpful key to unlocking his Gospel. If Matthew was written in Galilee, which seems probable, this provides an important interpretive key. It helps us understand that much of Matthew's unique content

was written for Jewish Christians suffering persecution in the synagogue community in Galilee. The location of the writing of Luke's Gospel (some scholars believe it was written in Ephesus as well) does not
have as big an impact on understanding his work. It is a key that doesn't
unlock as many doors.

If indeed John was written in Ephesus, as Ireneaus and Eusebius affirm, we would expect such a unique location to have an effect on the
content of the Gospel. If John is writing initially to Ephesian ears
(though his Gospel was quickly circulated throughout the Roman province of Asia and beyond), there are a number of expectations that come
to the surface. What would we expect of a Gospel written in a city like
Ephesus?

Ephesus was a city dominated by pagan temples. After Augustus el-
evated the city to the status of the capital of the province of Asia, Ephesus began to flourish. This was long before John relocated there. The city
was filled with temples dedicated to the worship of Rome, Augustus,
Livia (Augustus's wife), Tiberius and later to the Emperor Hadrian.
Emperor worship was one of the most important features of the life
situation of Ephesus.[4]

John's first readers, located in the center of emperor worship in the
Roman province of Asia, would have been extremely sensitive to any
claim Jesus or his followers would have made of him being the Son of
God. This was a title that belonged solely to the emperor. Also John's
lengthy presentation of Pilate, an appointee of Emperor Tiberius, would
have captured the imaginations of his first readers who passed Tiberius's
temple every day.

Without question the greatest pagan presence in Ephesus was the
cult of Artemis. Her temple, known as the Artemisium, four times the
size of the Parthenon, was on the top of every ancient list of the Seven
Wonders of the World. A local nativity myth even held that Artemis
had been born in Ephesus. The temple was destroyed and rebuilt more
than once, finally sinking into a swamp, only to be discovered in 1869,
thirty feet below ground.

The presence of the Artemisium, in effect, made Ephesus the pagan
sister city of Jerusalem. They were both temple cities. So committed was

the city to the goddess that she was regarded as "Artemis of the Ephesians." Not only did the cult of Artemis flourish there, an entire economy was based on the activity of the temple (see Acts 19:23-41). Centuries before Jesus overturned the tables of the moneychangers for the
first time in the temple in Jerusalem (Jn 2:12-22), the Artemisium had
been a "place of merchandise." For both Jerusalem and Ephesus, the
economy of the city was based on its temple.

When John used words like *Lord* or *Savior* in regard to Jesus, his
Ephesian readers would have recognized terms that, in their city, had
been applied to Artemis. His consistently negative use of the word
world (*kosmos*) would have also echoed in the ears of his Ephesian hear-
ers who had worshiped Artemis as the "Queen of the Cosmos."

One final connection between Ephesus and Jerusalem, which would
have had an impact on John's Gospel, was the substantial presence of a
Jewish community in the city. Though an estimate of its precise population has eluded scholars, there is abundant evidence of a thriving Jewish
community in Ephesus. Several inscriptions, primarily regarding fu-
neral arrangements, have been discovered that mention the fact that
coffins and other paraphernalia were paid for by Jewish citizens. Carved
into one of the steps of the famous Library of Celsus is the image of a
Jewish menorah.[5]

The greatest source of information on a Jewish presence in Ephesus
comes to us from Josephus. He records a number of Roman edicts concerning the Jewish community there. The Romans exempted the Jews in
Ephesus from military service and allowed them to keep all of their religious customs.[6] Most significant, the Jews in Ephesus were allowed to
continue to contribute to the upkeep of the temple in Jerusalem via the
temple tax.[7] Josephus tells us this resulted in tremendous tension between the other Ephesians and the Jewish community due to the fact
that so much income was being sent outside the city to another temple
besides the Artemisium.[8]

So John's first readers, many of whom were from the Jewish community in Ephesus, would have been ostracized by the Romans for refusing
to worship the emperor. Likewise, they would have been excluded from
their own Jewish community for worshiping Jesus of Nazareth (see

Acts 18:19-21; 19; 20:16; 1 Cor 15:32; 16:8).[9] John's presentation of Jesus as being consistently misunderstood and ridiculed, even by members of his own family, would have resonated with his first readers in Ephesus.

John's unique focus on the city of Jerusalem would have connected with his first listeners, who resided in a "temple city" of their own. Two-thirds of the action in John's account of the life of Jesus takes place in the holy city. John's Gospel has even been characterized as a "city story."[10] His experience of living in this well-known pagan sister city for over fifty years had a deep impact on the way he communicated all the various nuances of his portrayal of the life of Jesus. It affected both the way he wrote as well as the way his first listeners heard his Gospel.

MAJOR THEMES

THE MOTIF OF MISUNDERSTANDING

*W*henever you read through the Synoptics it is clear that Matthew, Mark and Luke display a strong dependence on the Law and the Prophets. Together they quote or allude to the first five books of Moses seventy times. They quote the Prophets seventy-four times. This is what we should expect given that the Law and Prophets are meant to prepare us to meet Jesus.

We might expect a similar dependence on the Wisdom books (Job, Psalms, Proverbs, Ecclesiastes, Song of Solomon), but surprisingly such is not the case. Matthew quotes the Wisdom writings seven times, Mark eight times and Luke only seven. This lack of dependence does not mean that the Wisdom books do not also prepare us to meet Jesus. In fact, we will see that they make us ready to meet him in an unexpected way.

"The Law, the Prophets and the Writings": this is a phrase with which we are familiar. It describes for us the three major sections of the Old Testament, but in Jesus' day this three-part structure wasn't fully established.

The Judaism of the time of Jesus wasn't a single unified entity. It was divided and subdivided. There were the priests, a hereditary group established by the law of Moses, as well as their associates, the Levites. There were the Sadducees, a powerful party that had purchased control from the Romans. (The Sadducees make no appearance in the Gospel of John.) There was a mysterious group referred to in the Gospels as the Herodians; we have no other reference to them in the ancient literature.

Some scholars see them as the vestiges of Herod the Great's political dynasty. More recently some scholars have begun to wonder if this is not the New Testament's name for the Essenes. It is striking that we find no reference to the numerous and powerful Essenes in the New Testament. Owing to the fact that Herod the Great gave his support and protection to the Essenes, it is not too far-fetched to posit that in Jesus' day they might have received the name of their former patron. There were developing radical terrorist groups like the Zealots and the Sicarii, who were hoping to overthrow the Roman oppressors. Finally, there were the Pharisees, the "separated ones." They were a back-to-the-Bible movement whose clout was based in the popular support they received from the people and the emerging rabbinic movement.

Our three-part designation for the Old Testament—the Law, Prophets and the Writings—was an idea we inherited from the Pharisees. They were the only group that embraced all three sections of the Old Testament. The Sadducees rejected the Prophets and the Wisdom writings; the Essenes were divided on the question. The issue of the three-part Old Testament was settled by the Pharisees around A.D. 90 in a rabbinic gathering known as the Council of Jamnia. After the distruction of the temple by the Romans in A.D. 70, the Pharisees were the only group left standing. The temple was gone; this effectively ended the role of the priests and Levites. Since the Sadducees powerbase was also the temple, they were out of the picture as well. The Essenes were virtually wiped out by the Romans, many of them crucified. It was left to the Pharisees to reform Judaism. They were allowed to relocate to the town of Jamnia (Javneh), where a group of rabbis led by Johannan ben Zakkai and Gamaliel II gave shape to the Judaism we know today. In the city of Jamnia the Pharisaic council established the final structure of the Law, the Prophets and the Writings as the accepted canon. It is no coincidence that in far-off Ephesus John was writing his Gospel at precisely the same time (c. A.D. 90).

John virtually bases his Gospel on the Wisdom books. He quotes or alludes to the Wisdom writings twenty-seven times. When the Synoptics tell of the second temple expulsion (Mt 21:12-17; Mk 11:12-19; Lk 19:45-48), Jesus has the words of the Prophets on his lips. When John provides his unique account of the first temple expulsion, the disciples find meaning for the event from the Psalms: "zeal for Your house will consume Me" (Jn 2:12-22; Ps 69:9).

If it is true that John bases his account of Jesus on the Wisdom writings, we might be tempted to simply say that for him Jesus is the Wisdom of God. And certainly this is true. But a closer look at the Wisdom books reveals a surprising, more pervasive theme: the inadequacy of Wisdom.

The book of Job is a novel about the inadequacy of the wisdom of Job's friends (and of Job himself!). When God finally appears at the end of the book, it is not with answers on his lips but with more unanswerable questions. The answer in Job is God himself showing up.

The psalms celebrate the power and wisdom of God surely, but numerically most of the songs are laments, which beg God to answer the deep and disturbing questions of human existence. As with Job, the answer in the psalms is the presence of God, his "showing up."

Ecclesiastes is the clearest portrayal of the inadequacy of wisdom in the Wisdom writings. Solomon, the wisest man who ever drew breath, laments again and again the vanity of wisdom (and wealth and power). The Song of Solomon celebrates something completely other than wisdom: romantic love. While Proverbs contains the greatest wealth of practical wisdom and some beautiful personifications of wisdom's captivating beauty, none of the Gospel writers refer to them.

If the strong underlying theme of the Wisdom writings is the inadequacy of wisdom, we should expect to see this theme reflected in John's Gospel. In fact, the inadequacy of wisdom is the fundamental theme of John's Gospel. Jesus is more than simply the Wisdom of God, he is the one who is constantly and consistently misunderstood. If God showing up is the answer in Job and the psalms, Jesus' incarnation, celebrated in John's high Christology, is the ultimate answer to every question for all time. Jesus will posit himself as the answer only in John's Gospel, via the "I am" sayings.

Each time Jesus reveals himself in John, he is phenomenally misunderstood. When he opens the door of the kingdom to Nicodemus and reveals the great mystery of the new birth, all the old man can utter is "How can these things be?" When Jesus appeals to the Samaritan woman at the well with the offer of the living water, which is really an offer of himself, all she can say is, "Is it because you don't have a bucket?" (see appendix B).

The motif of misunderstanding presents Jesus not as the great Teacher but as the misunderstood Messiah. As the Gospel progresses, Jesus will become increasingly lonely until finally, on the cross, he is all alone. His luminous answers were all misunderstood. (They will finally be comprehended only at the coming of the Holy Spirit [Jn 12:16; 14:25].)

THE PROPHET LIKE MOSES

"The Lord your God will raise up for you a prophet like me from among your own brothers. You must listen to him. . . . I will put My words in his mouth, and he will tell them everything I command him. I will hold accountable whoever does not listen to My words that he speaks in My name."

DEUTERONOMY 18:15, 17-19

Though John may be unique in his use of the Wisdom writings, this does not mean he disregards the rest of the Old Testament. The other principal theme of his Gospel is based on a passage from the book of Deuteronomy. It provides the basis for Jesus' self-understanding as the "Sent One" (Jn 4:34; 5:23, 30, 37; 6:38, 44; 7:16, 18, 28, 33; 8:16, 18, 26).

It is clear that Jesus' relationship with God is understood as a relationship to his Father. In John he refers to God as his Father 107 times. This degree of intimacy with God as Father gets Jesus into hot water more than once. In the Jewish world, to claim to be the Son of God was a claim to being equal with God (Jn 10:31-33).

A facet of Jesus' unique relationship with the Father that only John brings out is wrapped up in the prophecy of Deuteronomy 18. In response to the people's fear of God, he promises to send another prophet like Moses. By Jesus' day this individual was simply referred to as "the Prophet."

His likeness to Moses would be centered on two concepts; he would only say the things God told him to say, like Moses had done, and he would be the "Sent One," deriving his authority solely from the One who sent him.

In John's Gospel we first see the notion of "the Prophet" as an inves-

tigative committee of Pharisees confronts John the Baptist. It is important to the writer of the Gospel to make clear from the outset of his
story that the Baptist has no claim to this title, though he understands
himself as having been sent from God as well. Of the four times in
John's Gospel where the phrase "the Prophet" occurs, the first two are in
relation to John the Baptist (Jn 1:21, 25). The other occurrences come
later in the Gospel when twice the crowd affirms that Jesus is the
"Prophet" who is come into the world (Jn 6:14; 7:40).

The theme of the prophet like Moses is expressed in John's Gospel in
a multitude of ways. When Jesus is referred to as "the One Moses wrote
about" (Jn 1:45), the connection back to Deuteronomy 18 is evident. In
John 3:34 (during one of John's sermonic conclusions) when the statement is made that "the one whom God has sent speaks the words of
God" (NIV), the images define each other. This Sent One is the same one
who speaks the words of God (see appendix D).

In Jesus' mind, every aspect of his coming as the Prophet like Moses
was wrapped in humility and subordination. He speaks the words of the
Father: he seeks to please the One who sent him. It is not his teaching
but the Father's. His total dependency and reliance on the sufficiency of
the Father is grounded in the theme of the Prophet like Moses.

THE GOSPEL THAT WHISPERS

John is a pastor and a preacher. He is one of the few remaining eyewitnesses and the last of the Twelve. The uniqueness of the content of his
Gospel is not a product of a systematic reorganizing of the story of Jesus'
life as much as it is the result of decades of preaching and teaching the
material. The unique stories he presents, the structure of the seven miracles, the numerous omissions and substitutions: these are the stories that
held together over all those years. The themes of darkness and light are a
result of the filter of decades of time. These are the stories that lasted. The
incarnation was not simply some organizing theological principle, the
centerpiece of his high Christology; it was the theme of John's life. It was
the lens through which he focused and understood Jesus' life.

As the stories were told and retold, the gaps became more obvious.
Repeated questions from his listeners over time made John aware of the

background they needed to understand, words he needed to translate, eyewitness details that made the stories hold together. I can imagine the tone of his voice shifting with these asides. "It was about one hundred yards," he would say, placing his hand beside his mouth. "You know, Jews don't touch utensils belonging to Samaritans." "It was about ten in the morning."

John is the only Gospel that whispers this way. The translators often express this shift in tone by using parentheses. The other Gospels have parenthetical statements, but nothing like the Gospel of John. Matthew explains in chapter 27 that the place where Jesus was crucified, Golgotha, should be translated "the Place of the Skull." Mark uses this parenthetical device a few more times. Depending on the translation you use, Mark contains as many as fifteen parenthetical statements. They are evenly divided between statements that provide background information (e.g., "She was 12 years old" [Mk 5:42] or "as a result, He made all foods clean" [Mk 7:19]) and passages that translate unfamiliar terms (e.g., "which is translated, 'Little girl, I say to you, get up!'" [Mk 5:41] or "that is, the day before the Sabbath" [Mk 15:42]). The longest passage in Mark that might be considered parenthetical is in 7:3-4.

The Gospel of Luke contains as few as six parenthetical statements. (Once again the determination of what is parenthetical or not is a subjective decision made by the translator and is open to question.) In Luke 2:2 he explains that the census that brought Jesus' parents to Bethlehem happened while Quirinius was governor of Syria. His longest parenthetical statement is Luke 7:29-30. Here, in what is usually interpreted as an aside, Luke celebrates the fact that the tax collectors were acknowledging that God's way was right while the Pharisees were rejecting God's purposes. This is consistent with Luke's favorite theme concerning Jesus turning the world upside down.

None of the Gospels utilize the parenthetical aside to the degree that John does. Merrill Tenney, in his article "The Footnotes of John's Gospel," reckons that there are as many as fifty-nine examples of John speaking parenthetically. Tenney refers to these as "footnotes." As I seek to engage the text with my imagination, these asides are more like whisperings. John uses this device in a number of ways. As in the other

Gospels, frequently he provides a translation for his listeners who do not speak Hebrew or Latin. Often he is providing background information, the missing piece of the puzzle that he has come to recognize after having told the story a thousand times. Sometimes these whispered asides provide nothing more than eyewitness detail. (For a partial list of these whisperings in John's Gospel see appendix C.)

This use of parenthetical device makes John wonderfully present in his Gospel. He is beside us as we are reading, explaining, giving us details his experience has taught him need to be provided. It makes it easy to imagine that we are sitting at John's feet hearing not simply his rendition of the life of Jesus but experiencing his whisperings, his asides. His Gospel is more a living monologue than a written story.

So now let us take our place at the feet of the last living disciple of Jesus and listen with fully engaged imaginations to an account of that luminous life which no one else could possibly ever tell us.

JOHN 1

DABAR: THE MISUNDERSTOOD WORD

¹In the beginning was the Word,
and the Word was with God,
and the Word was God.
²He was with God in the beginning.
³All things were created through Him,
and apart from Him not one thing was created
that has been created.
⁴Life was in Him,
and that life was the light of men.
⁵That light shines in the darkness,
yet the darkness did not overcome it.

*T*he Gospel of John begins with a sermon that is a song. Arguably these are the greatest words ever written. Before they were scratched across the rough surface of a parchment, they were preached a thousand times, proclaimed in synagogues and on street corners. I imagine them echoing among the 137 columns of the Artemisium in Ephesus.

The opening verses, the prologue, contain the themes John will develop in his Gospel. Think of them as a lyrical table of contents. He will present blocks of material and then sum up what he has said in a sermonic conclusion. Familiarize yourself with the tone of his preaching and you will recognize it again and again. It echoes with his themes, with his high Christology. He is straining at the limits of language here, describing in "clumsy bricks" all that his eyes had seen, his ears had heard and his hands had actually touched!

The first two verses are bookended with the Genesis phrase *In the beginning*. The word *Word* (*logos*) occurs three times, as does the word *God* (*theos*). They are equal; they are the same. "In the beginning" also happens to be the Hebrew title of the book of Genesis (*bereshit*). The bookends of the Genesis phrase establish the Old Testament context of the prologue. It also provides the basis for understanding John's use of the word *logos*.

Volumes exist on the meaning and backgrounds of logos. More words have been spent defining *Word* than any other word. This gives a hint at how complicated these first two verses can be. The word *logos* came to have associations with a heresy that would become Gnosticism, whose early forms John is already fighting (1 Jn 4:2-3; 2 Jn 7). This early form of Gnosticism, known as Docetism (from *dokeo*, "to seem") taught that Jesus only "seemed" to come in the flesh. In his Gospel, John will fire the first broadside against Docetism in verse 14, where he will proclaim that the *logos* became flesh. But, and this is important, this does not mean that John has in mind the docetic idea of *logos* when he uses the word. Quite the contrary.

In Ephesus, the use of the word *logos* would have brought a world of different associations. When Ephesian ears heard the word, they would have immediately thought of Heraclitus, the sixth century B.C. philosopher. His father, Bloson, had been King of Ephesus. He was an ancient philosophical hometown hero. He developed his own unique concept that he referred to as the Logos. It would eventually be embraced by later Stoicism. Heraclitus's *logos* was a complicated concept that philosophers still debate. It represented fire, war, a world principle, even universal law. When, in Ephesus, John used the word *logos*, he could not have been unaware of the city's connection with Heraclitus. But, and this is also important, this does not mean that John had in mind the philosophy of Heraclitus when he used the word *logos*.

The bookends established it all. When John says "word," it is not the Greek logos but the Old Testament Hebrew *dabar* he has in mind. *Dabar* means both "word" and "deed." When God says something, it happens. For example, saying "let there be light" is how God creates light (Gen 1:3). If Jesus is the Word, in this sense, we would expect John to provide some similar examples:

- "your son will live" heals the royal official's son (Jn 4:50)
- "walk" causes the lame man to rise (Jn 5:11)
- "go" opens the eyes of the blind man (Jn 9:7)
- "come out" calls Lazarus from the tomb (Jn 11:43)

It is through the Word, the *Dabar* of God, that all creation happens: "the heavens were made by the word of the Lord" (Ps 33:6). This is a concept rooted in the Wisdom books on which John will base his presentation of Jesus (Ps 107:20; 147:18; 148:8). The conviction that Jesus is the creative power of God was basic to Paul's understanding of who Jesus was as well (Col 1:15-18; see Heb 1:2; Rev 19:13).

The Genesis bookends and the focus on creation make clear John's understanding and use of logos. He does not derive his understanding of the term from either Docetism or Hellenistic philosophy, but we can be certain that when he spoke, preached and finally wrote these opening words in a place like ancient Ephesus, he was aware of all of these associations. He is not drawing upon them or improvising in some way, he is taking the term back, reestablishing its true meaning from the Old Testament Scriptures.

In verse 4, as John strains with words to capture this Jesus he had known, two words come to his mind that perfectly describe him: *light* and *life*. God had spoken both light and life into being by means of his powerful *dabar*. The two are closely associated in the Wisdom books, which John uses as the basis of his Gospel (Job 3:20; 33:28, 30; Ps 36:9; 56:13; Prov 6:23; 16:15). For John, only Jesus is the source of eternal life (Jn 3:15, 36; 4:14; 5:21, 24, 26; 6:33, 40; 17:2). He is the life (Jn 11:25; 14:6) as well as the bread of life (Jn 6:35, 48) as well as the light of the world (Jn 8:12; 9:5; 12:46). He is the light of men (Jn 1:4).

Verse 5, the intermediate close of the opening sermon (John will resume preaching in verse 10), encapsulates the struggle of the whole of his Gospel. Throughout the remaining chapters, Jesus will shine, stubbornly, faithfully and obediently. It was his nature to do so. He will shine in the darkness that was the first-century world. Though that world will rally all its dark forces to extinguish the light that Jesus is, according to John, the darkness will fail. It will not overcome the light that is Jesus.

In our own time darker forces still struggle to overcome his light; larger more powerful kingdoms war against it. But if Jesus truly is all that John says he is, they too are predestined to fail.

THE "WITNESS/MARTYR"

⁶There was a man named John
who was sent from God.
⁷He came as a witness
to testify about the light,
so that all might believe through him.
⁸He was not the light,
but he came to testify about the light.
⁹The true light, who gives light to everyone,
was coming into the world.

*V*erse 6 represents the first example of John shifting from his preaching voice to his narrative voice. It is a momentary break in the sermon. Our English words *witness* and *martyr* are rooted in the same Greek word *martyrion*. John the Baptist was a living example of both. In the struggle between the light and darkness, Jesus has an ally, John the Baptist. He is there in every Gospel, as the forerunner of Jesus' ministry.

The three of them are actually cousins: John, the writer of the Gospel, John the Baptist and Jesus. The Baptist's mother, Elizabeth, was a relative of Jesus' mother, Mary (Lk 1:36). Two Johns: one preaching and writing, the other waiting, baptizing and prophesying.

Jesus does not begin his ministry in a vacuum but rather in a firestorm created by his cousin. John the Baptist is already under investigation by the Jewish authorities (Jn 1:22). He will eventually stir up trouble with Herod Antipas over Herod's adulterous marriage to his brother's wife. For this he will eventually become a martyr.

The firestorm Jesus enters is not the only trouble John stirred up. It is also a firestorm of renewed faith. In the splintered religious world that was first-century Judaism, John the Baptist had sounded a clarifying note of repentance, and the starving people had responded by the thousands. It was God's perfect preparation for the coming of the light to make people aware of the depth of the darkness in their own lives.

When verse 8 states that John the Baptist was not the light, it is only the first of a long list of denials. Again and again from his own lips John will deny that he is the Messiah. This is because there were a growing number of people who were convinced he was. Today there is still a small sect that worships John the Baptist as the Messiah, the Mandaeans. As the story of John unfolds in the Gospel, it is striking just how many times the Baptist pronounces his litany of denials. He is not the Prophet. He is not the light. He is not the Messiah. This is unique in all the Gospel portrayals of John the Baptist.

Acts 19:3 provides a clue to what is going on. Here Paul encountered a group of disciples who knew nothing about the Holy Spirit. When Paul asked them what kind of baptism they received, they responded "John's baptism." It is no coincidence that this all happened in the city of Ephesus. Could it be that group still existed, all these years later? John needs to repeat the Baptist's denials? The Baptist was not the light but merely a testimony to the light. The true light was coming, John writes, and the very thought of it causes him to burst once more into song.

THE SONG TO THE INCARNATION

[10] He was in the world,
and the world was created through Him,
yet the world did not recognize Him.
[11] He came to His own,
and His own people did not receive Him.
[12] But to all who did receive Him,
He gave them the right to be children of God,
to those who believe in His name,
[13] who were born,
not of blood,
or of the will of the flesh,
or of the will of man,
but of God.
[14] The Word became flesh,
and took up residence among us.
We observed His glory,
the glory as the One and Only Son from the Father,
full of grace and truth.

¹⁵(John testified concerning Him and exclaimed,
"This was the One of whom I said,
'The One coming after me has surpassed me,
because He existed before me.'")
¹⁶Indeed, we have all received grace after grace
from His fullness,
¹⁷for the law was given through Moses,
grace and truth came through Jesus Christ.
¹⁸No one has ever seen God.
The One and Only Son—
the One who is at the Father's side—
He has revealed Him.

*J*ohn's sermon resumes with a discord, an open fifth that is neither major nor minor. It will become a principle theme, one of the primary lenses through which he will understand Jesus' life. It is based on misunderstanding. For a person who had given so much of his life to understanding Jesus and helping others to do so, a nagging mystery remains:

• Though the light shines, it was not comprehended.

• The world was created by him, but it did not recognize him.

• Though he came to his own, his own did not receive him.

In a city of professional teachers, intellectual descendents of Heraclitus, John will present Jesus as the teacher no one was ever quite able to understand. Those who do receive and believe, however, will become God's own children, not born of flesh and blood but born by God's own doing. The passage modulates in verse 14. The opening phrase has been building since verse 1. It is not simply John's opening salvo against Docetism, although it certainly is that. In these four words John makes the single most remarkable statement regarding the nature of Jesus. It is the keystone to his high Christology: "The Word became flesh."

The One who was from the beginning, through whom God created everything, himself became a created being of flesh and blood, a body for a tent which for a while he pitched in the world—in John's world.

When he marvels "and we observed his glory," I hear a precise echo from his first letter and his breathless statement "what we have heard, what we have seen with our eyes, what we have observed and have touched with our hands" (1 Jn 1:1). The same hand must have written these very words.

In his opening verses John had spoken of Jesus in terms of light and life. Now he expands. The living One, who was light, was full of grace and truth. *Grace* (*charis*) is a word that reaches back to the Hebrew word *hesed.* It is the defining characteristic of God in the Old Testament. It is often translated "mercy," sometimes "love." The King James Version translates the word fourteen different ways, having to invent the word *lovingkindness.*

Though it is untranslatable, as the KJV difficulties reveal, a good working translation is captured in this sentence: "When the one from whom I have a right to expect nothing gives me everything."

And truth. Jesus is full of grace and truth, but not truth as anyone in the history of humankind has ever known. Not truth as a right answer or truth as the correct words, but truth as a person—living, breathing and eventually bleeding and dying. Truth that one comes to know personally in the context of a life, not between the pages of a textbook. From this moment on, knowing the truth will not necessarily mean being right but rather being faithful. Knowing the truth will no longer mean knowing the answers but only knowing Jesus Christ.

Verse 15 is an abrupt interruption both literarily and grammatically. First, John suddenly takes us back to the Jordan River and to the Baptist once more. Second, he is using a grammatical device known as the historical present tense. (The Holman Christian Standard Bible cited in this book has neglected to reflect this in its translation.)

The writer is gesticulating with words. John did not cry out long ago, he is crying this very moment, for the text should read "John cries out . . ." The curtain rises on the scene fresh every time the Gospel is read. And what is John shouting all of a sudden? What does he have to say that was so important as to interrupt the Evangelist's beautiful sermon? He is insisting again on his subordination to Jesus. Even though John was born approximately nine months before Jesus (see Lk 1:26, 56), he is shouting like a madman that Jesus existed before him. It is an echo back to verse 1, and neither of the Johns wants us to forget it.

After the abrupt interruption, John resumes his sermon. This will be the last refrain until John 3:13, so pay close attention. He's returned to the topic of grace and truth from verse 14. Jesus Christ is an overflowing grace, pouring out to us, he writes. The law, the *dabarim,* or "words," came through Moses. This is not a negative statement to John's Jewish readers, and it should not be to us. The law was good and perfect, the gift of God to his people. But, writes John, something unimaginably better has been granted by the same God, who was in the beginning, grace and truth.

THE VOICE IN THE WILDERNESS

[19]*This is John's testimony when the Jews from Jerusalem sent priests and Levites to ask him, "Who are you?"*

[20]*He did not refuse to answer, but he declared: "I am not the Messiah."*

[21]*"What then?" they asked him. "Are you Elijah?"*

"I am not," he said.

"Are you the Prophet?"

"No," he answered.

[22]*"Who are you, then?" they asked. "We need to give an answer to those who sent us. What can you tell us about yourself?"*

[23]*He said, "I am a voice of one crying out in the wilderness: Make straight the way of the Lord—just as Isaiah the prophet said."*

[24]*Now they had been sent from the Pharisees.* [25]*So they asked him, "Why then do you baptize if you aren't the Messiah, or Elijah, or the Prophet?"*

[26]*"I baptize with water," John answered them. "Someone stands among you, but you don't know Him.* [27]*He is the One coming after me, whose sandal strap I'm not worthy to untie."*

[28]*All this happened in Bethany across the Jordan, where John was baptizing.*

*T*he song comes to an abrupt end and we are back on the other side of the Jordan with John and the investigative committee from Jerusalem.

In verse 8 the sermon told us that John was not the light. Now we will hear it from his own lips.

The Sadducees represent the real power in Jerusalem. The priests and Levites press John to reveal his true identity, though we will discover in verse 24 that the Pharisees are also involved. He affirms he is not the Messiah. This would've been their greatest fear since the Messiah, any messiah, would threaten the power of their handlers back at the temple, the high priests. Neither is John Elijah, the one who would come before the anointed one, according to Malachi 4.

Both in Matthew 11:2-19 and Mark 9:11-13, Jesus will affirm that indeed John is the Elijah who was to come, that he had come in the spirit and power of the prophet, from the place of Elijah, with the clothing of Elijah, with the message of Elijah. The Levites suspect John might be an actual reincarnation of the prophet, which he clearly is not.

Finally they ask, "Are you the Prophet?" To which John will answer no for the third time. They are referring to the individual prophesied in Deuteronomy 18. The complete designation is "a prophet like [Moses]." In Deuteronomy, God promised to send another prophet like Moses (see the introduction). Like Moses, he would only speak the words that God had told him to speak. He would be a one-on-one authoritative representative, like the Hebrew *shaliah*.[1] It is vital that John's readers hear from the Baptist that he lays no claim to any of these titles. In Ephesus there was still apparently a sizable group of John's followers (Acts 19:1-7). John is formally divesting himself of any sort of claim. He is not the Messiah. That title uniquely belongs to his cousin Jesus, who is waiting just behind the curtain. Though he might reasonably claim the title of Elijah, he refuses it. It is vital that we hear from his lips that he lays no claim to being the Prophet, since this will become a key in the Gospel to understanding the true nature of Jesus, who is the unique spokesperson sent by the Father.

If the Baptist is none of these, then just who is he? Verse 22 creates a tone of expectation. The committee must return with an answer. John's solitary voice breaks the pregnant pause. He understands his calling on the basis of Isaiah 40:3, the very verse on which the Essenes based their self-understanding. Given the fact that he has just refused all their grandiose titles, I insert the word *only* in his response. "I am only a voice of one crying out . . ." I imagine John looking beyond them: "in the wilderness: Make straight the way of the Lord." He is hoarse and tired. He does not have much longer to live.

The question in verse 25 concerning baptism seems to be predicated on the fact that the Pharisees had also been part of the group that sent the investigating committee. They would have been concerned with any observance regarding purity, since 90 percent of their oral tradition was concerned with ritual purity. John's baptism is confusing to them. In a world of works righteousness, anything having to do with repentance can be confusing. They understand ritual oblation for purity, and they understand baptizing Gentile converts into Judaism. But John's baptism is neither of these. He is performing what in essence is a one-time ritual baptism of repentance (Mt 3:11; Mk 1:4). What's most confusing, he is baptizing Jews. In John 3:25 we will see John's disciples arguing with a solitary Jew over the issue of "ceremonial washing," another indication of the confusion surrounding John's ministry of baptism.

If John is not the Messiah, Elijah or the Prophet, then why is he baptizing? He responds simply that he baptizes with water. Then, ominously, he whispers, "Someone stands among you . . ." Is Jesus there in the crowd at that very moment? After all, he will appear the next day. If Jesus is there, he hears John's most humble confession that he is not worthy to untie the sandal of the one who is coming after him.

As the rabbinic movement was gaining momentum, some of the leaders became concerned that some students were becoming a bit too worshipful of their teachers. And so a mandate was issued: "All services which a slave does for his master will a pupil do for his teacher, with the exception of undoing his shoes."[2]

John's humility becomes crystal clear in light of these words. He is not worthy to be either a slave or the pupil of the One who is coming. Yet the humility of the One who is coming will embrace even more than the untying of the sandal. Unimaginably, he will even wash the feet of his own disciples (Jn 13). And only John's Gospel will tell us that story.

THE UNKNOWN LAMB

²⁹The next day John saw Jesus coming toward him and said, "Here is the Lamb of God, who takes away the sin of the world! ³⁰This is the One I told you about: 'After me comes a man who has surpassed me, because He existed before me.' ³¹I didn't know Him, but I came baptizing with water so He might be revealed to Israel."

³²And John testified, "I watched the Spirit descending from heaven like a dove, and He rested on Him. ³³I didn't know Him, but He who sent me to baptize with water told me, 'The One you see the Spirit descending and resting on—He is the One who baptizes with the Holy Spirit.' ³⁴I have seen and testified that He is the Son of God!"

*T*his section begins a miraculous week in the life of Jesus. The first day was John 1:19-28, where John the Baptist gave his testimony as to who Jesus is and what he means. The next day begins here with verse 29. If we count backwards from the last day (Jn 2:1), which is identified as the "third day" or Tuesday, this would be the Sabbath. (Another reconstruction places the Sabbath between the end of chapter 1 and the beginning of chapter 2.)

According to Luke 3:23, Jesus is approximately thirty years old, which would make the year sometime between A.D. 24 and 26, accounting for the misalignment of the calendar in the sixth century by Dionysius Exiguus. Tiberius has been emperor since A.D. 14. Caiaphas has been high priest since A.D. 18. Pontius Pilate has just been appointed governor of Judea (c. A.D. 26). All the players are in position for the most remarkable story that will ever unfold.

When John the Baptist exclaims that Jesus is the "Lamb of God," the Old Testament begins to resonate. The Passover lamb of Exodus 12 is in view. (Passover is actually near [see Jn 2:13].) The prophet Isaiah had said the Messiah would be led like a lamb to the slaughter (Is 53:7). Today Jesus will take his first steps toward fulfilling Isaiah's prophecy. Of all the host of associations that might be made (e.g., 1 Pet 1:19; Rev 5:6), Jesus being the Lamb of God represents the fact that God himself is going to provide a sacrifice, a lamb, just as Abraham had hoped he would in Genesis 22:8, when he was being asked to make his son the sacrifice. Now, in fulfillment of that image of the father offering his own son, God himself will provide Jesus to be the lamb, our sacrifice. It perfectly fulfills our working definition of the Hebrew word *hesed*: "when the person from whom I have a right to expect nothing gives me everything."

Verse 31 echoes and reinforces the motif of misunderstanding so central to John's presentation of Jesus. Even John the Baptist, who had leaped in his mother's womb, did not know who his cousin Jesus truly was, not until he saw the Spirit come down and rest on him. (Notice that the actual baptism of Jesus is omitted! Apparently the author of the Gospel trusts that his readers have already read that account in one of the Synoptics.)

As the Gospel unfolds, Jesus will reveal himself as the sent One, and his Father as the One who had sent him. In verse 33 John too sees himself as one who has been sent to baptize with water. The One who had sent John had told him that the sign of the Holy Spirit remaining on Jesus would provide the proof that Jesus would baptize not with water but with the Holy Spirit. His closing words set the trajectory for the rest of the story. By what he had seen and what he'd been told by God, the Sender, John gives the testimony that Jesus is the Son of God.

THE PROMISE OF A NEW NAME

³⁵Again the next day, John was standing with two of his disciples. ³⁶When he saw Jesus passing by, he said, "Look! The Lamb of God!"

³⁷The two disciples heard him say this and followed Jesus. ³⁸When Jesus turned and noticed them following Him, He asked them, "What are you looking for?"

They said to Him, "Rabbi" (which means "Teacher"), "where are You staying?"

³⁹"Come and you'll see," He replied. So they went and saw where He was staying, and they stayed with Him that day. It was about 10 in the morning.

⁴⁰Andrew, Simon Peter's brother, was one of the two who heard John and followed Him. ⁴¹He first found his own brother Simon and told him, "We have found the Messiah!" (which means "Anointed One"), ⁴²and he brought Simon to Jesus.

When Jesus saw him, He said, "You are Simon, son of John. You will be called Cephas" (which means "Rock").

Without John's Gospel we would be left to believe that Jesus' call to the disciples had come at their first meeting (Mt 4:18-22; Mk 1:14-20; Lk 5:1-11). John lets us know they had spent time together before that call came. We will see that whenever he omits a block of material, like the calling of the first disciples, he will always substitute fresh material not found in the Synoptics.

It all begins the "next day" when Jesus is seen passing by the crowd that has gathered around the Baptist. Two of his disciples hear John repeat the words he had spoken the day before, that Jesus is the Lamb of God. Upon hearing these words John's disciples began to follow Jesus. One of them is identified as Andrew (v. 40). The other we can only guess is John himself, the writer of the Gospel. He will never identify himself in the text, only his disciples will spell out who he is in John 21:20, 24.

In verse 38 Jesus speaks his first words of the Gospel. Seeing that he is being followed, he asks "What do you want?" Imagine hearing these words addressed to you from Jesus himself, for that is exactly what John wants you to experience. How would you reply to such a question? What do you want from Jesus? Ask yourself.

It is probably John himself who blurts out, "Rabbi, where are You staying?" Of all he might have asked for, the youthful John can only manage this. It is significant that at this point the translation of the Hebrew word *rabbi* is given. In Jesus' day, in the midst of an emerging rabbinic movement, the definition of the word was still in flux. Literally, it means "great" or "good" one. By the time John writes his Gospel the meaning of the term has solidified to mean "teacher." Jesus' response is as simple as John's question. "Come and see."

This scene comes to a close with a frustrating lack of detail. We would love to know precisely where Jesus was staying. According to verse 43 we can guess that they are still in the vicinity where John had been baptizing the day before, since in verse 43 Jesus "leaves for Galilee." When John concludes that they spent the day with Jesus, even providing the exact time, we must recognize an eyewitness detail. It serves no purpose in the narrative apart from allowing us to "be there." Since time was normally reckoned by counting the hours from sunrise (approximately 6 a.m.), the tenth hour would be around 4 p.m. It appears they spent the rest of the day together, and though we would give a treasure to know the course of their conversation, we never will.

Since verse 39 represents the close of the day, we can only guess that verses 40-42 represent the following day. Notice that Andrew is identified as "Simon Peter's brother," although we have not yet met Simon, nor has he been nicknamed Peter. Andrew, once a follower of the Baptist and now a follower of Jesus, goes to find his brother Simon.

It is striking that only John's Gospel uses the Hebrew word *Messiah*, and then only twice, here and in John 4:25. (Many modern translations will substitute *Messiah* for the Greek word *Christ* [*christos*].) John will whisper the translation into the Greek for us, "Christ." Both terms should be understood as fluid; that is, they filled the shape of a number of different hopes and dreams. For some the Messiah is a spiritual figure. For others he is a political leader. There are countless shades of meaning in between the two. We have already seen the priests and Levites struggling with the term, guessing that John must be the Messiah simply because he was baptizing. (*Messiah* means "anointed one.") Jesus will not strictly condemn the use of the title in regard to himself, though again and again he will tell people to keep the term a secret. Only after his transfiguration, as he begins his final journey to Jerusalem and the cross, will he begin to define the word for his disciples: that the Messiah is the one who will suffer, die and be raised on the third day.

Verse 42 may very well be the first time Jesus and Peter had ever laid eyes on each other. Here John will use a special word only found twice in the New Testament and uniquely used to describe the way Jesus looks at Peter (see Lk 22:61). The word is *emblepo*, which means "gaze upon." I think it functions in the narrative here to slow down time. There is a pause as Jesus looks intently at the person who will become without question his closest friend. Speaking in the present tense, Jesus says "You are Simon." He shifts to the future when he says "You will be called Cephas," which John whispers is translated "Rock." The shift is significant because it speaks of a moment in the future when Simon will earn his nickname by confessing that Jesus is the Christ (Mt 16:18). At that future moment Jesus will proclaim, in the present tense, "You are Peter." In John 2:25 John will tell us that Jesus knows what is in a person's heart without having to be told. This is the first example.

Revelation 2:17 speaks of a time when we will each be handed a white stone on which will be written a new name. It has been said that that name will perfectly describe who we truly are. I cannot help but believe that Cephas, the rock, was Simon's "white stone name." It perfectly describes who he would eventually become.

A LADDER TO HEAVEN

43The next day He decided to leave for Galilee. Jesus found Philip and told him, "Follow Me!"

44Now Philip was from Bethsaida, the hometown of Andrew and Peter. 45Philip found Nathanael, and told him, "We have found the One Moses wrote about in the Law (and so did the prophets): Jesus the son of Joseph, from Nazareth!"

46"Can anything good come out of Nazareth?" Nathanael asked him.

"Come and see," Philip answered.

47Then Jesus saw Nathanael coming toward Him and said about him, "Here is a true Israelite; no deceit is in him."

48"How do you know me?" Nathanael asked.

"Before Philip called you, when you were under the fig tree, I saw you," Jesus answered.

49"Rabbi," Nathanael replied, "You are the Son of God! You are the King of Israel!"

50Jesus responded to him, "Do you believe only because I told you I saw you under the fig tree? You will see greater things than this." 51Then He said, "I assure you: You will see heaven opened and the angels of God ascending and descending on the Son of Man."

*U*ntil this moment, Jesus has been fairly unintentional, responding to John's question, wordlessly experiencing the pronouncements of the

Baptist. Now he becomes more deliberate. He "decided" to leave for Galilee and "found" Philip, which implies that he looked for him. Philip will appear in three more significant scenes in John's Gospel (Jn 6:5-7; 12:21-22; 14:8-9). (In the Synoptics his name is only listed among the Twelve.)

For the first time in John's Gospel, Jesus issues the command (not the invitation) to "Follow me." Not a single detail is given. We are left to suppose that Philip responded in obedience, since immediately we see him finding Nathanael. John provides the detail that Philip, Andrew and Peter are from the town of Bethsaida, though it will appear later that they have relocated to Capernaum.

The exchange between Philip and Nathanael seems straightforward. "We have found the one Moses wrote about in the Law: . . . Jesus . . . from Nazareth," Philip blurts out. Notice he avoids the term *Messiah*. Nathanael's response is completely negative. He represents those who were "Jesus' own," but who would not recognize him (Jn 1:11). His response, "Can any good thing come out of Nazareth?" reveals the common attitude toward Nazareth in particular and the area of Galilee in general. The fact that Nathanael himself is from Cana in Galilee (Jn 21:2) makes the statement all the more remarkable. When we realize that those words were spoken by a fellow Galilean, we understand that they do not represent a scathing comment from Nathanael but rather a sad statement of common opinion.

Philip responds with Jesus' same words from verse 39, "Come and see." That simple response sets up one of the most remarkable exchanges in John's Gospel. The excited Philip, with a pessimistic Nathanael in tow, makes his way to Jesus. When Jesus sees them approaching, he who does not need to be told about a person refers to Nathanael as a "true Israelite" in whom there is no deceit. Jesus' graceful response to Nathanael is in stark contrast to Nathanael's original negative opinion of Jesus.

Jesus' compliment appears to make Nathanael somewhat suspicious. He wonders out loud how Jesus can know him. Jesus' response in verse 48 could not appear to be more ordinary. He saw Nathanael under a fig tree before Philip called him. But what happens between verses 48-49 can only be described as an explosion of faith.

Nathanael gasps, "Rabbi," which John no longer needs to translate, "you are the Son of God." The person whom Jesus described as the true Israelite concludes, "You are the king of Israel."

In verse 50 even Jesus seems surprised at Nathanael's abrupt turn-around. He believes simply because Jesus said he had seen him under an ordinary fig tree? He will someday see something far more extraordinary; he will witness heaven open and the angels ascending and descending on the Son of Man.

John's remarkable story leaves us scratching our heads wondering what in the world just happened. This would be a good place for John to whisper some explanation in our ears, but he remains frustratingly silent. He wants us to engage with the text with our own imaginations.

All the pieces of the puzzle are there. When Jesus says of Nathanael that there is no deceit in him, if we are paying attention we should think of Jacob, the man of deceit in the Old Testament. Is Jesus setting up a contrast?

Next we have the business of the mysterious explosion of faith in response to what seems an ordinary statement from Jesus. Here the detail of the fig tree becomes important. The fig tree is a symbol of Israel and eventually became used as a place of prayer in Jesus' time.[3] This leads us to tentatively conclude that Nathanael might have been at prayer under the fig tree when Philip called him. When we add to this scenario the fact that the Pharisees had reawakened the hope of the coming of the Messiah to the extent that asking for his return was considered a necessary part of every prayer, the scene comes into focus.

Perhaps Nathanael was at prayer, since he was under the fig tree, a place of prayer. If indeed he was a true Israelite, as Jesus said, he must've been praying for the coming of the Messiah when Philip interrupted him. This accounts for his extraordinary response to Jesus' seemingly ordinary statement.

Finally, what are we to do with Jesus' statement about heaven opening and the angels ascending and descending on the Son of Man? This takes us back to the image of Jacob, the man of deceit. He experienced a dream in Genesis 28 that involved a ladder that went to heaven, upon

which angels were going up and down. Could it be that Jesus is imply-
ing that what Jacob could only dream about, a way to heaven, Nathanael
and the others would actually someday see: that Jesus is Jacob's dream
come true!

JOHN 2

FIRST UNMIRACULOUS MIRACLE

¹On the third day a wedding took place in Cana of Galilee. Jesus' mother was there, and ²Jesus and His disciples were invited to the wedding as well. ³When the wine ran out, Jesus' mother told Him, "They don't have any wine."

⁴"What has this concern of yours to do with Me, woman?" Jesus asked. "My hour has not yet come."

⁵"Do whatever He tells you," His mother told the servants.

⁶Now six stone water jars had been set there for Jewish purification. Each contained 20 or 30 gallons.

⁷"Fill the jars with water," Jesus told them. So they filled them to the brim. ⁸Then He said to them, "Now draw some out and take it to the chief servant." And they did.

⁹When the chief servant tasted the water (after it had become wine), he did not know where it came from—though the servants who had drawn the water knew. He called the groom ¹⁰and told him, "Everyone sets out the fine wine first, then, after people have drunk freely, the inferior. But you have kept the fine wine until now."

¹¹Jesus performed this first sign in Cana of Galilee. He displayed His glory, and His disciples believed in Him.

*I*t is the final day of that first miraculous week and Jesus will conclude on the third day with one of his most unmiraculous miracles.

There has been all sorts of speculation regarding the wedding feast at Cana. Some believe it might actually have been John's wedding. He seems to have inside information, and Mary, his aunt, appears to take a special interest in the faux pas of running out of wine. For the first time it has occurred to me that perhaps it is Nathanael's wedding. It happens in Cana, and he is described as having been from Cana (Jn 21:2). The story occurs in the text right after we have met Nathanael for the first time. Could he have also been praying about his upcoming marriage when Jesus interrupted him? Did he invite Jesus to the wedding as Matthew had immediately invited Jesus to his home for a grand banquet (Mt 9:9-13)? The truth is no one knows, but it is an interesting exercise of the imagination trying to put the pieces of the puzzle together.

The exchange between Jesus and his mother is the most interesting example we have of their mature relationship. She is concerned that the wine is gone, and perhaps someone she loves is going to be embarrassed. Her son does not see that he has anything to do with the situation. Wherever Jesus says his "time has not yet come," it implies that the time is coming for him. The cross is still almost three years away.

What fascinates me is that in their interplay Mary understands that Jesus' response is not a no. This becomes clear when she immediately tells the servants (*diakonois*) to "do whatever he tells you."

The six water jars are specifically made of stone because stone does not pass on uncleanness. Vessels for ritual oblation were always made of stone. Their total capacity is 180 gallons! This equals 900 fifths of wine. If we conservatively value this excellent wine at $30 a bottle, the total comes to $27,000.

This, Jesus' first miracle, is also his least miraculous. The miraculous transformation occurs between verses 7-8. Jesus tells the servants to fill the jars and then to take it to the toastmaster (literally the "master of the three couches"). That is it—did you miss it? The toastmaster tastes the water that had been turned into wine and comments on the host's unorthodox behavior. You were supposed to serve the best wine first, when the guests' palettes are still receptive to its quality. But you, he explains, "have saved the best till now."

John closes the scene by whispering an explanation to us. This was Jesus' first miraculous sign, performed in Cana of Galilee. This is how he revealed his glory, and his disciples put their faith in him.

"This is how he revealed his glory"—this is Jesus' idea of a miraculous sign, one known only to the servants. There was no waving of arms, no calling attention to himself. Jesus simply takes the water of the old orthodoxy and unassumingly transforms it into the wine of the new reality. His other miracles in John will fit the same pattern, except for one:

- In chapter 4 he will heal the official's son in absentia.

- In chapter 5 he will cause the lame to walk by simply saying "get up." This man does not even know Jesus' name.

- In chapter 6 he will feed five thousand by simply pronouncing the blessing over the meal.

- Also in chapter 6 he will walk on the water. Mark observes that he was walking past them, his purpose simply to get to the other side of the lake (Mk 6:48).
- In chapter 9 he will heal the blind man, also in absentia.

The single exception of the rule in regard to Jesus' unmiraculous miracles is the raising of Lazarus in chapter 11. This he accomplishes by means of a loud shout.

Finally, we need to take into account John's first Ephesian readers. When they hear of Jesus' first miracle, their minds would immediately turn to the god Dionysius. (The Romans called him Bacchus.) On more than one occasion his myth includes stories of Dionysius turning water into wine. There was a large cult in Ephesus dedicated to Dionysius: his image is even found on the mosaic floor of one of the wealthy homes. In their minds they must have understood the story as proof that Jesus had power to take back from the pagan world the illusion of its power to transform. Dionysius was a myth. Jesus was a flesh and blood man known to John himself, who had witnessed in real life Jesus' power and glory.

A VIOLENT BOOKEND

12 After this, He went down to Capernaum, together with His mother, His brothers, and His disciples, and they stayed there only a few days.

13 The Jewish Passover was near, so Jesus went up to Jerusalem. 14 In the temple complex He found people selling oxen, sheep, and doves, and He also found the moneychangers sitting there. 15 After making a whip out of cords, He drove everyone out of the temple complex with their sheep and oxen. He also poured out the moneychangers' coins and overturned the tables. 16 He told those who were selling doves, "Get these things out of here! Stop turning My Father's house into a marketplace!"

17 And His disciples remembered that it is written: Zeal for Your house will consume Me.

18 So the Jews replied to Him, "What sign of authority will You show us for doing these things?"

19 Jesus answered, "Destroy this sanctuary, and I will raise it up in three days."

20Therefore the Jews said, "This sanctuary took 46 years to build, and will You raise it up in three days?"

21But He was speaking about the sanctuary of His body. 22So when He was raised from the dead, His disciples remembered that He had said this. And they believed the Scripture and the statement Jesus had made.

23While He was in Jerusalem at the Passover Festival, many trusted in His name when they saw the signs He was doing. 24Jesus, however, would not entrust Himself to them, since He knew them all 25and because He did not need anyone to testify about man; for He Himself knew what was in man.

Whenever we come across a story in John that is unique (and 92 percent of his Gospel is unique!), it is always a good idea to check what is going on at roughly the same place in Matthew, Mark and Luke. Inevitably John is omitting material from the Synoptics and substituting fresh information we would have never known otherwise. It provides an opportunity to see his mind at work.

Roughly at this point in the Synoptics we would be reading of the temptation of Jesus in the wilderness. But John leaves the significant block of material out. Instead he substitutes the first temple expulsion. Later in the narrative where the second temple expulsion is presented by the Synoptics, John omits that story and substitutes the coming of the Greeks (Jn 12:20-22). It is as if John wants us to be reminded that there are many different wilderness experiences. While some are literally in the desert, a deeper, lonelier wilderness can be experienced in a crowded place where worship should be offered but tragically is not.

From Cana, Jesus and his family, along with his disciples, returned to Capernaum. In all the other Gospels Capernaum becomes Jesus' base of operations during the Galilean segment of his ministry. John tells us he stayed there for a few days. Hopefully he rested.

It is a long journey from Capernaum down the Jordan Valley and up the steep ridge to Jerusalem. Though Passover occurs in the spring, it can still be an incredibly hot journey.

The Pharisees' oral law maintained that everyone within a prescribed distance of Jerusalem had to physically come to the city itself for the three great feasts: the Shalosh Regalim. They are Pentecost, Tabernacles and Passover. Scholars speculate that the population of Jerusalem would skyrocket from approximately 250,000 to over one million. It is crowded; more to the point, in the divided time of Jesus it is a powder keg. The Roman governor would journey to Jerusalem from his capital in Caesarea hoping his presence with the addition of his legionaries, would keep the peace, the Pax Romana. Jesus is going to severely test that hope.

The marketplace for the temple, referred to as the Bazaar of Annas, was normally set up on the Mount of Olives.[1] John's story is the first reference to it being moved into the temple precincts. This might explain Jesus' surprise and rage seeing it there in the Court of the Gentiles. John lists the various departments in the holy shopping mall. There are three sources of sacrificial animals: cattle, sheep and doves. Then there are the moneychangers. They are providing a service by exchanging various local currencies for the Tyrian shekel, which was accepted in the temple due to its higher silver content and the fact that it was closest to the old Hebrew shekel in value. Only a small percentage that covered physical wear to the coins was added, so Jesus' anger is not because they are gouging the people.[2] His particular anger is directed in verse 16 to the dove sellers. Doves were the sacrifice provided for the poor. When Jesus is dedicated in the temple, his parents had to offer doves (Lk 2:24). Having driven the cattle and sheep from the temple with a homemade whip (only John's account refers to the whip) and overturned the tables of the moneychangers, Jesus focuses his indignation on the dove sellers. He makes an allusion to Zechariah 14:21, a passage that speaks of a time when tradesmen will no longer be allowed in the temple.

It is significant that in John's unique portrayal of this unique first temple expulsion, Jesus' disciples find meaning in the event by means of a passage from the Wisdom writings. For them Psalm 69:9 illuminates the otherwise confusing and upsetting incident. This particular psalm prophetically speaks of the crucifixion and looks forward to the moment when Jesus will be offered sour wine vinegar to drink while he is on the cross. Why has Jesus done such a dangerous thing? Because it was written that "Zeal for Your house will consume Me."

Listen carefully to the question of the shocked Jews. They do not ask why Jesus had made a wreck of their market; they only ask for a sign to prove that he has the authority to have done it. No one seems to question if what Jesus did by twice tearing up the temple marketplace was the right or wrong thing to do. The fact is, it was a very pharisaic thing to have done.

In verse 19 Jesus gives his answer. It is veiled and vague, and in light of the motif of misunderstanding they will completely misunderstand the point. Jesus' pronouncement may very well be the reason John substituted this story. At this moment, so early in the ministry, what Jesus says will three years later be the basis for the charge that will result in his crucifixion, that he spoke of tearing down the temple (see Mt 26:61; 27:40; Mk 14:58; 15:29). In Acts 6:14, it will also be the reason for the stoning of Stephen. It is said of him that he followed the one who spoke against the temple.

It may be impossible for us to imagine just how precious the temple was to the Jews of Jesus' time. The Talmud says, "he who has not seen the Temple of Herod has never seen a beautiful building."[3]

The vast thirty-five-acre complex, still under construction, would have been one of the Seven Wonders of the World had it existed when Herodotus first made his list. John's first Ephesian readers lived in the city that boasted of the Temple of Artemis (which actually was one of the Seven Wonders of the World). They would've understood the Jews' attachment to the temple of Herod and perhaps would have been especially shocked at first by the story of what Jesus had done. (In Acts 19 Paul will cause a similar disturbance regarding the temple in Ephesus.)

Jesus has uttered a deeply spiritual truth regarding his crucifixion and resurrection. In John's Gospel we will learn to expect that the immediate response of the crowd will be not a simple but a gross misunderstanding of what he has said. And that is exactly what happens next.

The Jews respond that it has taken forty-six years to build the temple. That would make the year A.D. 27, which fits the timeline perfectly. The temple had been begun by Herod in the eighteenth year of his reign (20 B.C.). The truth is, it will not be finished for another forty-three years, until A.D. 64, only to be completely destroyed by Titus in A.D. 70. They have missed the true meaning of his pronouncement, and it is not difficult to understand why.

Verse 21 provides an example of John's unique backward-looking perspective. He is whispering again, explaining to his listeners that this is what Jesus actually meant, for chances are we would have misunderstood him as well. Jesus was referring to his body and the fact that it would come alive again after three days. His disciples remembered all of this later, after it happened, and they believed. John records for us in John 20:8 the precise moment this happened to him, when he looked into the empty tomb on resurrection morning.

In verses 23-25 John is speaking into your ear, explaining, summing up this first block of time in Jerusalem. Many saw the signs Jesus performed in Jerusalem, although John has not provided any miraculous stories for us, unless he is referring to Jesus' miraculous courage in the temple. In John 4:45 his Galilean neighbors celebrate what Jesus had done when he returns home.

Versus 24-25 are a parentheses inside a parentheses. The statement, connected to the past week in Jerusalem, also looks ahead to the next encounter with a man named Nicodemus.

JOHN 3

THE REBIRTH OF AN OLD MAN

3:1–21

THE *SHOSHBIN*

3:22–36

THE REBIRTH OF AN OLD MAN

¹There was a man from the Pharisees named Nicodemus, a ruler of the Jews. ²This man came to Him at night and said, "Rabbi, we know that You have come from God as a teacher, for no one could perform these signs You do unless God were with him."

³Jesus replied, "I assure you: Unless someone is born again, he cannot see the kingdom of God."

⁴"But how can anyone be born when he is old?" Nicodemus asked Him. "Can he enter his mother's womb a second time and be born?"

⁵Jesus answered, "I assure you: Unless someone is born of water and the Spirit, he cannot enter the kingdom of God. ⁶Whatever is born of the flesh is flesh, and whatever is born of the Spirit is spirit. ⁷Do not be amazed that I told you that you must be born again. ⁸The wind blows where it pleases, and you hear its sound, but you don't know where it comes from or where it is going. So it is with everyone born of the Spirit."

⁹"How can these things be?" asked Nicodemus.

¹⁰"Are you a teacher of Israel and don't know these things?" Jesus replied. ¹¹"I assure you: We speak what We know and We testify to what We have seen, but you do not accept Our testimony. ¹²If I have told you about things that happen on earth and you don't believe, how will you believe if I tell you about things of heaven? ¹³No one has ascended into heaven except the One who descended from heaven—the Son of Man. ¹⁴Just as Moses lifted up the snake in the wilderness, so the Son of Man must be lifted up, ¹⁵so that everyone who believes in Him will have eternal life.

¹⁶"For God loved the world in this way: He gave His One and Only Son, so that everyone who believes in Him will not perish but have eternal life. ¹⁷For God did not send His Son into the world that He might condemn the world, but that the world might be saved through Him. ¹⁸Anyone who believes in Him is not condemned, but anyone who does not believe is already condemned, because he has not believed in the name of the One and Only Son of God.

¹⁹"This, then, is the judgment: The light has come into the world, and people loved darkness rather than the light because their deeds were evil. ²⁰For everyone who practices wicked things hates the light and avoids it, so that his

deeds may not be exposed. ²¹But anyone who lives by the truth comes to the
light, so that his works may be shown to be accomplished by God."

*H*e is extremely powerful and undoubtedly wealthy, perhaps one of
the richest men in Jerusalem. He is a member of the Sanhedrin, our
closest parallel to the Supreme Court.[1] He is also a Pharisee, a member of one of the back-to-the-Bible movements that was gaining tremendous popular support in Jesus' time. They would eventually be the
reformers of Judaism. Our view of the Pharisees has been twisted due
to the fact that most of the Pharisees we meet in the Gospels are part
of a relatively small group who hounded Jesus at almost every step.
Nicodemus gives us a unique opportunity to see what most of their
number were really like: earnest, seeking men who loved God and the
Torah passionately.[2]

That he bears a Greek name speaks of how completely Hellenized
Judaism had become. Nicodemus means "victorious people" and probably speaks of the hopes and dreams of his parents.

It is often preached that Nicodemus came to Jesus at night because
he was somehow embarrassed or afraid of associating with him in public. This idea does not hold up for two reasons. First, the rabbis reserved
the evening hours for biblical discussion. Second, Nicodemus is not a
cowardly person. In John 19:38-39, he will appear with Joseph of Arimathea, probably another follower of Hillel, to claim the body of Jesus,
thereby identifying himself with a known criminal. This is hardly the
behavior of a cowardly man.

He appears to be speaking for the Sanhedrin, or at least the contingent within when he says "we." He speaks for all of Judaism when he
expresses the notion that Jesus must be a teacher from God because of
what he is doing, that is, performing miraculous signs (see Jn 2:23). But
faith based on signs is no faith at all.

Jesus' response seems to come out of nowhere. He begins his pronouncement with the mysterious "amen, amen," his unique and unprece-
dented way of signaling that he is about to say something of utmost
importance. You will not see the kingdom of God unless you are born

again, he says. Nicodemus wanted to talk about what Jesus had been doing. Jesus only wants to talk about what God is doing, giving birth to sons and daughters in the kingdom. The only time the phrase *born again* was used in Judaism it refered to Gentiles who became full proselytes. Then it was said a person was born again. To make his point in an extreme and over-the-top way, one rabbi argued that a man who was born again could actually marry his own mother, since he was now a totally different person. (Please understand he was not suggesting that this actually be done, but only making the point about the power of rebirth.) Nicodemus, with his keen mind, seems to understand that Jesus is not talking about mere proselyte baptism.

A deeply spiritual statement made by Jesus will always give rise to a profound misunderstanding in John's Gospel. Nicodemus's response seems especially obtuse. He is stuck. Jesus will attempt to draw him out. He begins with another solemn "amen, amen." The birth he refers to happens through water and Spirit. *Water* is a spiritually charged term in John, with all sorts of connotations. Baptism and birth are only two of them. Water has healing associations (Jn 5:2; 9:7) as well as divine associations (Jn 6:19). Jesus' first miracle involved water (Jn 2:7). When Jesus is crucified, only John refers to the water that flows from the wound in his side (Jn 19:34). Most often water in John's Gospel is connected to the identity of Jesus and the promise of new life through the Spirit. Of the twenty times John uses the word *water*, more than all the other Gospels combined, nine of those occur in the story of the Samaritan woman at the well (Jn 4:1-26). The most striking pronouncement in regard to water comes in John 7:37 when Jesus says if a person is thirsty they must come to him and drink. The water is a symbol of what Jesus promises to provide. In his last long discussion with the disciples, Jesus will make it clear that this promised provision will be the Holy Spirit (Jn 16:1-16).

In this light, Jesus' statement about water and the Spirit is repetitive, like his "amen, amen." A person must be born of the water *that is* the Spirit, the unique promise and provision of Jesus. Only he makes entering the kingdom possible. Verse 6 confirms that he is speaking of spiritual birth and not the "waters" of physical birth.

The "you" of verse 7 is plural. Jesus is addressing Nicodemus and all of his powerful friends: "You all should not be surprised." What follows is a beautiful play on words that works both in Hebrew and Greek. In Greek the word *pneuma* means both Spirit and wind. The same is true of the Hebrew word *ruah*. The Spirit, which is like water, is also like wind. You can hear it and see its effect, but it remains invisible. You cannot see where it is coming from or where it is going. Nicodemus came thinking he knew what God was doing by virtue of what he saw in the signs. Jesus is pointing to a vastly deeper, invisible movement of God. He is inviting the old man to enter into the mystery of this new birth. This is an invitation that Nicodemus would eventually respond to. But for now his world is spinning. Jesus has pulled the rug out from under his old orthodoxy. All he can do is mutter, "How can this be?"

In verse 10 the "you" is singular. Jesus is focusing on Nicodemus. "Teacher of Israel" was a technical term for a Pharisee. They referred to themselves as the "teachers of Israel." Frankly, Nicodemus should have understood the radical new birth, which Jesus has been speaking about. It is spoken of in Ezekiel 36:26. You can feel Jesus' frustration. He has spoken and testified, but "you" (v. 11; now it is plural once more) refused to accept it. He has spoken in terms of wind and water and birth, earthly images meant to make clear the truth.

A sermon, one of John's sermonic conclusions, is coming, and the only question is, Does it begin with verse 13 (as I tend to believe it does) or verse 16? I hear the tone shift to that of a sermon in verse 13. It is the language of one of his motifs: the ascending-descending motif we first saw in John 1:51 (see Jn 6:62; 20:17; see Prov 30:4). Before Jesus will ascend to heaven, John preaches, he must be "lifted up," which is always a metaphor for crucifixion (see Jn 12:32).

The image, preached a thousand times, comes from the book of Numbers 21:4-9 and the story of the serpents in the wilderness. As the people of Israel were traveling toward the Red Sea, they became impatient and once more began to grumble. They spoke out against both God and Moses, complaining about the manna, saying they detested it. In response, God sent venomous serpents into the camp. Many were bitten and died as a result. Acknowledging their sin, in repentance the people asked that the snakes be taken away. When Moses came to the Lord he was told to make an image of a serpent and place it on a pole, telling the people that all who looked at the serpent would be healed. It was an image that had been burned into the collective memory of Israel (see 2 Kings 18:4).

Just as Moses had "lifted up" the serpent, in the same way the Son of Man will be lifted up. ("Lifted up" and "stretched out" were two of the most common metaphors for crucifixion.) Like the Israelites in the wilderness, anyone who is willing to look to that cross in obedience and faith will be healed.

John's Ephesian readers would have had a different image in their imaginations when they heard of the serpent on the pole. In the heart of the city of Ephesus was the temple to Asclepius, the God of healing. His symbol was a staff with a serpent wrapped around it. Live serpents were released in the temple at night while the sick were left sleeping on the floor. In the morning they would report their dreams to the priest who would then prescribe a cure, which usually included a trip to one of the local bath houses. Again we see the connection to water and healing.

John's first listeners would have understood once more that the power for true healing was being reclaimed exclusively by Jesus, even as he had robbed Dionysius of his power.[3]

With verse 16, John's sermonic conclusion begins in earnest. This is definitely John's voice and without a doubt not his whispering voice. Verses 16-18 are the most quoted words from the New Testament.

It was for love that God gave his Son. Like the Israelites in the wilderness, whoever believes in the Son will not perish but will live forever. The bite of the serpent will lose its power as we look to Jesus "lifted up" on the cross. God did not send Jesus to condemn but to save. Jesus will repeat this idea at least three more times (Jn 5:22; 8:15; 12:47). Note that "condemn" and "judge" represent the same Greek word, *krine*.

Verse 19 opens with "This, then, is the judgment" ("This is the verdict" [NIV]). John will reach all the way back to the prologue and the image of the misunderstood light, summing up everything to the discussion of the new birth. Nicodemus is still standing on the stage. So far in John's story he is the exemplar of the one who lives by the truth and comes into the light.

THE *SHOSHBIN*

²²*After this, Jesus and His disciples went to the Judean countryside, where He spent time with them and baptized.* ²³*John also was baptizing in Aenon near Salim, because there was plenty of water there. People were coming and being baptized,* ²⁴*since John had not yet been thrown into prison.*

²⁵*Then a dispute arose between John's disciples and a Jew about purification.* ²⁶*So they came to John and told him, "Rabbi, the One you testified about, and who was with you across the Jordan, is baptizing—and everyone is flocking to Him."*

²⁷*John responded, "No one can receive a single thing unless it's given to him from heaven.* ²⁸*You yourselves can testify that I said, 'I am not the Messiah, but I've been sent ahead of Him.'* ²⁹*He who has the bride is the groom. But the groom's friend, who stands by and listens for him, rejoices greatly at the groom's voice. So this joy of mine is complete.* ³⁰*He must increase, but I must decrease."*

³¹*The One who comes from above is above all. The one who is from the earth is earthly and speaks in earthly terms. The One who comes from heaven is above all.* ³²*He testifies to what He has seen and heard, yet no one accepts His testimony.* ³³*The one who has accepted His testimony has affirmed that God is true.* ³⁴*For God sent Him, and He speaks God's words, since He gives the Spirit without measure.* ³⁵*The Father loves the Son and has given all things into His hands.* ³⁶*The one who believes in the Son has eternal life, but the one who refuses to believe in the Son will not see life; instead, the wrath of God remains on him.*

*J*esus' first visit to Jerusalem during his ministry is now over. He has confronted the powers that be while redemptively engaging with one of its most powerful representatives. The seed has been sown and now it is time to move on. He goes out into the countryside with his disciples to a place John refers to as Aenon, a word which simply means "springs." We are not sure of its precise location. Because there was an abundance of water there, his disciples were baptizing. In 4:2, John is careful to tell us that Jesus himself did not baptize people, only his disciples did. Perhaps he is trying not to appear as simply another John the Baptist.

Eusebius makes much of verse 24. For him it explains the difference between John and the Synoptics. John gives an account of Jesus' ministry before the imprisonment of John the Baptist. The Synoptics tell what occurred after. According to Eusebius this explains the uniqueness of John.[4] Surely this explanation is insufficient to cover all the differences between John and the Synoptics.

John assumes we already know the details of the Baptist's arrest and imprisonment. The Jews are still trying to harmonize what John's baptism really means. As they gather together, an argument is brewing concerning ceremonial washing. Someone must have been reasoning that the baptism of John was merely another form of ritual oblation. The fact that the disciples of Jesus are also now baptizing only made the confusion worse.

Finally, they come to John for help. The fact that they refer to him as rabbi provides a clue to the fact that the term is still in flux. John's ministry is strikingly different from that of a typical rabbi in many ways. Perhaps here the use of the term more reflects the original meaning of "great one."

The crowd assumes that John should be upset that he is losing followers to Jesus. "Everyone is flocking to Him," they exclaim in verse 26. The occasion provides one last opportunity for John to deny any claim to being the Messiah. The group in Ephesus who still follow John the Baptist must hear and understand this message. John is not the Christ but only the one who was sent before him.

Very much the rabbi, John concludes with a little parable. Jesus is like the bridegroom. John is the best man; in Judaism, the *shoshbin*. The bride, represented in part by the people who are leaving John and following Jesus, belongs only to the bridegroom. It is right that they should follow Jesus, just as Andrew had walked away from John the Baptist months before.

The *shoshbin* was given a very specific task: to guard the bride until the bridegroom returned from the wedding feast. In a time where kidnapping brides was still a viable threat, the one person who could be trusted to guard her was the bridegroom's best friend, the *shoshbin*. After delivering her safely to the bridal chamber, it was his responsibility to wait outside in the dark, keeping watch. He especially would be able to recognize the familiar voice of the bridegroom in the dark, allowing him to enter the chamber to be with his bride. Then, according to custom, he would "go away rejoicing." It is the particular joy of the man who has witnessed his best friend finally finding the woman he loves. John says that specific joy now belongs to him. He will, in effect, move off into the darkness now, leaving Jesus with his bride.

As this poignant scene closes, the writer of the Gospel steps back onto the stage with another "summing up" sermon. He begins by affirming that Jesus is indeed the One who is from above. John, on the other hand, belongs to the earth. It is a theme he has been reinforcing since chapter 1. Twice he proclaims that Jesus is "above all." In verse 34 he provides another affirmation that Jesus is the Prophet like Moses; he is sent from God and speaks only the words of God. John is summing up and preparing for all that is to come. In Jesus, everything is at stake. God has limitlessly given him the Spirit, has placed everything in his hands. It is all there for the person who will simply look to him and be healed, who will put their faith in him.

JOHN 4

MISUNDERSTOOD WATER

4:1–42

MIRACLE IN ABSENTIA

4:43-54

MISUNDERSTOOD WATER

¹When Jesus knew that the Pharisees heard He was making and baptizing more disciples than John ²(though Jesus Himself was not baptizing, but His disciples were), ³He left Judea and went again to Galilee. ⁴He had to travel through Samaria, ⁵so He came to a town of Samaria called Sychar near the property that Jacob had given his son Joseph. ⁶Jacob's well was there, and Jesus, worn out from His journey, sat down at the well. It was about six in the evening.

⁷A woman of Samaria came to draw water.

"Give Me a drink," Jesus said to her, ⁸for His disciples had gone into town to buy food.

⁹"How is it that You, a Jew, ask for a drink from me, a Samaritan woman?" she asked Him. For Jews do not associate with Samaritans.

¹⁰Jesus answered, "If you knew the gift of God, and who is saying to you, 'Give Me a drink,' you would ask Him, and He would give you living water."

¹¹"Sir," said the woman, "You don't even have a bucket, and the well is deep. So where do You get this 'living water'? ¹²You aren't greater than our father Jacob, are You? He gave us the well and drank from it himself, as did his sons and livestock."

¹³Jesus said, "Everyone who drinks from this water will get thirsty again. ¹⁴But whoever drinks from the water that I will give him will never get thirsty again—ever! In fact, the water I will give him will become a well of water springing up within him for eternal life."

¹⁵"Sir," the woman said to Him, "give me this water so I won't get thirsty and come here to draw water."

¹⁶"Go call your husband," He told her, "and come back here."

¹⁷"I don't have a husband," she answered.

"You have correctly said, 'I don't have a husband,'" Jesus said. ¹⁸"For you've had five husbands, and the man you now have is not your husband. What you have said is true."

¹⁹"Sir," the woman replied, "I see that You are a prophet. ²⁰Our Fathers worshiped on this mountain, yet you Jews say that the place to worship is in Jerusalem."

²¹Jesus told her, "Believe Me, woman, an hour is coming when you will worship the Father neither on this mountain nor in Jerusalem. ²²*You Sa-maritans worship what you do not know. We worship what we do know, because salvation is from the Jews.* ²³*But an hour is coming, and is now here, when the true worshipers will worship the Father in spirit and truth. Yes, the Father wants such people to worship Him.* ²⁴*God is spirit, and those who worship Him must worship in spirit and truth."*

²⁵*The woman said to Him, "I know that Messiah is coming" (who is called Christ). "When He comes, He will explain everything to us."*

²⁶*"I am He," Jesus told her, "the One speaking to you."*

²⁷*Just then His disciples arrived, and they were amazed that He was talk-ing with a woman. Yet no one said, "What do You want?" or "Why are You talking with her?"*

²⁸*Then the woman left her water jar, went into town, and told the men,* ²⁹*"Come, see a man who told me everything I ever did! Could this be the Messiah?"* ³⁰*They left the town and made their way to Him.*

³¹*In the meantime the disciples kept urging Him, "Rabbi, eat something."*

³²*But He said, "I have food to eat that you don't know about."*

³³*The disciples said to one another, "Could someone have brought Him something to eat?"*

³⁴*"My food is to do the will of Him who sent Me and to finish His work," Jesus told them.* ³⁵*"Don't you say, 'There are still four more months, then comes the harvest'? Listen to what I'm telling you: Open your eyes and look at the fields, for they are ready for harvest.* ³⁶*The reaper is already receiving pay and gathering fruit for eternal life, so the sower and reaper can rejoice together.* ³⁷*For in this case the saying is true: 'One sows and another reaps.'* ³⁸*I sent you to reap what you didn't labor for; others have labored, and you have benefited from their labor."*

³⁹*Now many Samaritans from that town believed in Him because of what the woman said when she testified, "He told me everything I ever did."* ⁴⁰*Therefore, when the Samaritans came to Him, they asked Him to stay with them, and He stayed there two days.* ⁴¹*Many more believed because of what He said.* ⁴²*And they told the woman, "We no longer believe because of what you said, for we have heard for ourselves and know that this really is the Savior of the world."*

*T*he opening statement of chapter 4 provides a small insight into Jesus'
motivation. He finds out that the Pharisees have heard his ministry is
becoming more successful than John's, that he is attracting more disciples than John, and so he leaves Judea and heads back north to Galilee.
The interesting twist is not that Jesus simply realized the success of his
ministry and left to avoid any competitive feelings. It has already been
made abundantly clear that John the Baptist understands he was not
Jesus' competitor. To the contrary, John is undoubtedly rejoicing in the
success of Jesus. Rather the point is, Jesus moves on because the Pharisees have heard about his success in relation to John. He does not want
to give their opponents any reason to cause friction between his disciples and John's.

As Jesus makes his way to Galilee he must pass through Samaria. It
is sometimes said that his willingness to go through the despised country of the Samaritans was a mark of Jesus' compassion. While there is
absolutely no question whatsoever in regard to Jesus' compassion, the
truth is that Galileans routinely passed through Samaria, according to
Josephus.[1] This misunderstanding is a result of superimposing Judean
Judaism over Galilean Judaism. There were significant differences. Besides the fact that Judean Jews looked down on their neighbors to the
north, Galilean Jews were known to consume meat and milk products
at the same time, something a strictly observant Jew would never do. It
seems Galileans also observed the traditions of the diaspora community
as well, celebrating Passover on Thursday instead of Friday night. Olive
oil from Galilee was considered unclean in Judea. In later years Galileans were not allowed to perform the public readings of Scripture in
Judean synagogues. On the whole the Galileans were considered more
lax in their observance.

The location of the well, just outside Sychar, is charged with historical
significance (Gen 29; 33; 48:22; Josh 24:32). The Samaritan woman will
refer to its history in verse 12. It is noon, the hottest part of the day, a
suspicious time to be drawing water. Beside this very historical well, history is about to be made again.

Jesus sends his disciples into town to buy food and sits down by the well to rest. After his long walk, he is tired and thirsty. When the woman comes to the well, Jesus makes a reasonable request. She has a bucket and he has none. Could she give him some water to drink?

The woman seems to take offense. Perhaps, with her history of woundedness, she would have responded to any man by pushing back. But Jesus is not just any man. The prejudice comes from her side, but it is a result of centuries of mutual hatred. Rabbi Eliezer, who was roughly contemporary with Jesus, said, "He that eats the bread of the Samaritans is like the one who eats the flesh of swine."[2]

Jesus' response is inviting. If she only knew . . . Though he is still thirsty, he offers her living water. It is a deeply spiritual invitation for which she has done nothing. Nothing except allowing Jesus to continue being thirsty.

In response to his offer of living water, she counters with practicality (he has no bucket) and gritty religious references. Who does he think he is? Does he think he is greater than the one who gave the well to her people in the first place? If you listen closely, you can still detect the tone of a wounded person.

Jesus is relentless in his spiritual pursuit. The water from the well will always leave one thirsty. His water is different. Once you drink it in, you will never be thirsty, and what's more a spring of living water will well up within you (see Jn 6:58, where Jesus makes the same point in regard to the manna).

There is a subterranean shift in her tone. Deep down there is an openness that was not there a moment ago. Though her statement still might be laced with sarcasm, she seems to be opening up slowly. She has begun to ask questions.

Jesus engages her in an unexpected way, as he did with Nicodemus. It was an entirely appropriate request to ask her to go and bring back her husband, to which she answers, "I don't have a husband."

This was not a deception. I imagine her responding to Jesus with a downcast expression. The tone of his response is full of compassion, not "I told you so" self-satisfaction.

She has had five husbands, when the rabbis had declared that three was the limit. The heartbreaking truth is that she is living with a man now who does not love her enough to make her his wife. I sense Jesus is sadly agreeing with her. A genuine relationship based on trust is slowly developing between the two.

In verse 19 her hope begins to rise. She perceives that there is something different about Jesus. She concludes he is a prophet. But old habits are hard to break and again she throws religious sand in his face, bringing up the schism between the Jews and Samaritans.[3]

Jesus will not be drawn into an argument. What he is talking about has nothing to do with Jerusalem or Gerizim. He has come to announce what the Father is doing (like his discussion with Nicodemus about the new birth that the Father makes possible by what he does). It is not about a place of worship, even an ordained place like the temple in Jerusalem. The good news is that the Father has come, actively seeking men and women who will worship in spirit and truth. Spirit is not bound to one location, and truth is not limited to one people group or denomination.

In verse 25 her voice begins to brim with expectation, even excitement. She knows the Messiah is coming. The Samaritans' special name for him was *Taheb*, the Revealer. She expresses the uniquely Samaritan hope of a Christ who will come and explain or reveal everything.

It is almost as if Jesus is finishing her sentence for her by this time. Literally he responds "I am," perhaps he is manifesting the divine name of God (Ex 3:14). Look closely at the response of the Twelve as they return with food from town. They are not surprised that Jesus is talking to a Samaritan. That would have been a common enough occurrence for a Galilean. They are surprised that Jesus is talking to a woman. Perhaps the deep division between men and women in Jesus' day was as deeply engrained as the schism between the Samaritans and the Jews. In general men did not speak to their wives in public. Rabbinic opinion against women was even more severe. "Better that the law be burned then delivered to a woman" was a well-known statement of the rabbis. The Pharisees said, "each time a man looks at the woman, he inherits Gehinnom."[4] Interesting though, as unorthodox as Jesus' actions might have been, no one has the courage to question him. Perhaps the disciples are beginning to discover that underneath the old orthodoxy Jesus is living out a new reality.

The message she takes back to town is consistent with the excitement of her words in verse 25. She reports that Jesus had told her everything about her life, the shame and hurt seemed to have vanished. "Could this be . . . ?" she exclaims. As the townspeople make their way to the well, John cuts back to the scene of Jesus and the Twelve.

They had left him exhausted and thirsty. Apparently the woman never responded to Jesus' thirst by giving him something to drink. He was too busy responding to her need. He doesn't seem to be tired any longer, and when the disciples offer him food he pushes it aside. He has been fed by the satisfying experience with the woman. In the wilderness temptation, Jesus had confronted the evil one by saying, "Man does not live on bread alone but on every word that comes from the mouth of God." The scene enacted beside the well is a living parable of the truth.

To Jesus' deeply spiritual statement the disciples responded, "Could someone have brought Him something to eat?" (v. 33). It is the motif of misunderstanding again.

Obedience is what nourishes Jesus. He is fed by finishing the work of the One who sent him. He quotes an ancient proverb about the harvest. It was meant to teach that there is no need to hurry, after all there are four months until the harvest. But nothing could be further from the truth. The fields are white. The heads of grain are bowed down. The reaper has already been paid and is moving out into the fields (compare Amos 9:13; Rev 14:15). Jesus' excitement at the thought of the harvest, of the work he has been sent to do, parallels the excitement of the woman who represents that harvest.

The Synoptics show Jesus being rejected by the Samaritans (Lk 9:51-56). John, so bent on providing the untold story of Jesus, shows him being accepted there. Many Samaritans believe simply because of the excited testimony of a woman, perhaps even because of the radical change in her countenance. Others come to believe as a result of spending time with Jesus, whom they welcomed for two days.

MIRACLE IN ABSENTIA

43After two days He left there for Galilee. 44Jesus Himself testified that a prophet has no honor in his own country. 45When they entered Galilee, the

Galileans welcomed Him because they had seen everything He did in Jerusa-
lem during the festival. For they also had gone to the festival.

⁴⁶Then He went again to Cana of Galilee, where He had turned the water
into wine. There was a certain royal official whose son was ill at Capernaum.
⁴⁷When this man heard that Jesus had come from Judea into Galilee, he went
to Him and pleaded with Him to come down and heal his son, for he was
about to die.

⁴⁸Jesus told him, "Unless you people see signs and wonders, you will not
believe."

⁴⁹"Sir," the official said to Him, "come down before my boy dies!"

⁵⁰"Go," Jesus told him, "your son will live." The man believed what Jesus
said to him and departed.

⁵¹While he was still going down, his slaves met him saying that his boy
was alive. ⁵²He asked them at what time he got better. "Yesterday at seven in
the morning the fever left him," they answered. ⁵³The father realized this was
the very hour at which Jesus had told him, "Your son will live." Then he him-
self believed, along with his whole household.

⁵⁴This, therefore, was the second sign Jesus performed after He came from
Judea to Galilee.

*A*fter the two-day delay, Jesus resumes his trip to Galilee. In verse
44 John whispers in our ear that Jesus had made it a point to say that a
prophet has no honor in his own country. The Synoptics use the statement to introduce a story of Jesus being rejected in Galilee (Mt 13:57;
Mk 6:4; Lk 4:24). John uses it to introduce a scene of Jesus being well
received in Galilee.

We are not told why he returns to Cana. Does he go back to the
house where his first unmiraculous miracle was performed? Does he
have family there? Does Nathanael, who is from Cana (21:2), have some
business there? Regardless, word spread all the way to Capernaum that
Jesus had returned from Jerusalem.

The nameless man who runs some twenty miles from Capernaum to
Cana to find Jesus is described as a "royal official" (*basilikos*). He is probably in the employ of Herod Antipas, perhaps he oversees tax collection

in the area of Capernaum, which was a large and prosperous city. If this is true, he would have certainly known Matthew. The official's son is dying and, desperate for help, the man has come to beg Jesus to come and heal his boy.

Verse 48 seems spoken under his breath. Jesus is frustrated that signs and wonders are necessary for people to believe. But the official seems to panic. Jesus must come with him, and he must come now!

This is another unmiraculous miracle, a miracle in absentia. All Jesus says is "Go, your son will live." There is almost always a miracle behind the unmiraculous miracles of Jesus. On this occasion it is the faith of the father, whose panicked desperation vanishes, replaced by belief. The miracle is that he took Jesus at his word without seeing the proof. The miracle is that he believed before he saw.

On his way back home, he is met by his slaves with the good news he already knows. His son has been healed. Precisely at 1 p.m., when he heard Jesus speak the promise that his son would be healed, twenty miles away his little boy got better.

An official from Herod Antipas and his entire household, that is, all of his family and slaves, believe in Jesus. They represent more of the ripe harvest Jesus had just spoken of to his disciples. Jesus is obediently finishing the work his Father sent him to do. And he is nourished all the more through his obedience. The miracle is not the point; it never is. The harvest is all that matters.

JOHN 5

HEALING WATERS

¹After this, a Jewish festival took place, and Jesus went up to Jerusalem. ²By the Sheep Gate in Jerusalem there is a pool, called Bethesda in Hebrew, which has five colonnades. ³Within these lay a large number of the sick— blind, lame, and paralyzed [—waiting for the moving of the water, ⁴because an angel would go down into the pool from time to time and stir up the water. Then the first one who got in after the water was stirred up recovered from whatever ailment he had].

⁵One man was there who had been sick for 38 years. ⁶When Jesus saw him lying there and knew he had already been there a long time, He said to him, "Do you want to get well?"

⁷"Sir," the sick man answered, "I don't have a man to put me into the pool when the water is stirred up, but while I'm coming, someone goes down ahead of me."

⁸"Get up," Jesus told him, "pick up your mat and walk!" ⁹Instantly the man got well, picked up his mat, and started to walk.

Now that day was the Sabbath, ¹⁰so the Jews said to the man who had been healed, "This is the Sabbath! It's illegal for you to pick up your mat."

¹¹He replied, "The man who made me well told me, 'Pick up your mat and walk.'"

¹²"Who is this man who told you, 'Pick up your mat and walk'?" they asked. ¹³But the man who was cured did not know who it was, because Jesus had slipped away into the crowd that was there.

¹⁴After this, Jesus found him in the temple complex and said to him, "See, you are well. Do not sin anymore, so that something worse doesn't happen to you." ¹⁵The man went and reported to the Jews that it was Jesus who had made him well.

*O*ne uniqueness of John's Gospel is his use of extended stories that center around a single individual: Nathanael, Nicodemus, the Samaritan woman, the woman taken in adultery, the man born blind and Lazarus. If you've ever spent time with an elderly person, you will notice their memories tend to focus on people as much or more than events. Perhaps this feature of John's Gospel points to his aged imagination.

We are told that Jesus is back in Jerusalem for an undisclosed feast. Only John shows us Jesus coming and going to Jerusalem on numerous occasions. The Synoptics focus on his final trip to Jerusalem.

John introduces the story by setting the scene with a detailed description of the pool of Bethesda. In contrast to the pool of Siloam, which was shallow and relatively small, the pool of Bethesda was the size of a football field and over twenty feet deep. It was located a stone's throw away from the temple. Today it is called the pool of Saint Anne, though in fact there is no longer an actual pool there.

Once again the story centers on the notion of the healing power associated with water in the ancient world. A great number of disabled people gathered there for healing. Verse 4 sounds like a scribal note of explanation that was incorporated into later copies of John. It does not exist in earlier manuscripts. It puts forth the notion that the people were waiting on the side of the pool for the water to be miraculously stirred. The notion has been put forth that the stirring of the water might have been caused by the bubbles of a subterranean spring. However this pool was not fed by springs but rather was a catchment basin.

Amid this crowd, we are told, there lies a man who for thirty-eight years had been an invalid. I call him the "man of excuses" because every time he speaks he makes a rather lame excuse. He is not a likable man. John's portrayal leaves us room to come to this conclusion on our own. He will provide a stark contrast to the very lovable man who was born blind (Jn 9).

Politically correct ears will burn at Jesus' initial question, "Do you want to get well?" It sounds unfeeling coming from someone like Jesus. But we need to remember that regardless of how it feels, if it is coming from Jesus, we can be certain it is the perfect question. As the story progresses we will realize that there is a very strong possibility that this man does not want to get well.

His first response, like all of his following responses, is a flimsy excuse. Most often all that stands between Jesus and us is a flimsy excuse. People, he says, keep getting in front of him and no one will help him into the pool and its healing waters. His first response makes me suspicious that after thirty-eight years his disability has become his identity. After all, we all tend to cling to our disabilities.

Jesus understands that there is no point in engaging with this man. If he is ever to walk again he must simply be commanded to do so. Because Jesus, in his humility, so often says, "it is your faith that healed you" (compare Mk 10:52; Lk 18:42), some have taught that a person must have faith in Jesus to be healed. This story flies in the face of that erroneous idea. The man has no idea who he is talking to. In a moment we will learn that he does not even know Jesus' name.

Jesus possesses a raw power and authority that is sometimes disturbing. When he says "Get up" to a total stranger, who by the way has not gotten up for thirty-eight years, there seems to be no choice but to obey. The man of excuses stands up and, in obedience to Jesus, picks up the mat he had been lying on.

The second part of verse 9 sounds the ominous note that all this took place on the Sabbath. Whenever that detail is given in the Gospels, you can be certain that Jesus is about to get into trouble for breaking an oral tradition of the Pharisees. When the Jews respond, the Old Testament is not the basis for their objection, but their oral law. The Pharisees had outlined thirty-nine different classes of forbidden work on the Sabbath.[1] By commanding the man to pick up and carry his mat, Jesus had violated one of the most basic of the oral laws.

For the second time the man speaks (v. 11), and for the second time he utters an excuse. It is not his fault that he is breaking the law: "the man who made me well" told me to do it. When they ask who this person is, we discover that the man of excuses hadn't even taken the time to learn the name of the person who had healed him.

A case can be made for this being another of Jesus' unmiraculous miracles. It was accomplished by the very ordinary command, "Get up." There was no waving of arms. Nothing about the way Jesus performs this miracle apparently attracted any attention. If this is true, then we should expect to find a miracle behind the miracle. Verse 14 provides that miracle—if we have the eyes to see it. It is described in three simple words, "Jesus found him." First, this implies that Jesus had looked for him. It was not enough for Jesus that the man had been healed of thirty-eight years of paralysis. Jesus had not come to simply give healing. He had come to give himself. And that is the miracle behind the miracle.

Jesus healed the man, sought him out and introduced himself. Of all that his awesome power and authority is capable of, in this case, it is powerless to change the man's heart. Having learned Jesus' name, the man of excuses goes to Jesus' persecutors and tells them who had commanded him to break their law. The result will mean persecution for Jesus (v. 16) and eventually the determination that he must die (v. 18).

THE PROPHET

16Therefore, the Jews began persecuting Jesus because He was doing these things on the Sabbath. 17But Jesus responded to them, "My Father is still working, and I am working also." 18This is why the Jews began trying all the more to kill Him: Not only was He breaking the Sabbath, but He was even calling God His own Father, making Himself equal with God.

19Then Jesus replied, "I assure you: The Son is not able to do anything on His own, but only what He sees the Father doing. For whatever the Father does, the Son also does these things in the same way. 20For the Father loves the Son and shows Him everything He is doing, and He will show Him greater works than these so that you will be amazed. 21And just as the Father raises the dead and gives them life, so the Son also gives life to anyone He wants to. 22The Father, in fact, judges no one but has given all judgment to the Son, 23so that all people will honor the Son just as they honor the Father. Anyone who does not honor the Son does not honor the Father who sent Him.

24"I assure you: Anyone who hears My word and believes Him who sent Me has eternal life and will not come under judgment but has passed from death to life.

25"I assure you: An hour is coming, and is now here, when the dead will hear the voice of the Son of God, and those who hear will live. 26For just as the Father has life in Himself, so also He has granted to the Son to have life in Himself. 27And He has granted Him the right to pass judgment, because He is the Son of Man. 28Do not be amazed at this, because a time is coming when all who are in the graves will hear His voice 29and come out—those who have done good things, to the resurrection of life, but those who have done wicked things, to the resurrection of judgment.

³⁰"I can do nothing on My own. I judge only as I hear, and My judgment is righteous, because I do not seek My own will, but the will of Him who sent Me.

³¹"If I testify about Myself, My testimony is not valid. ³²There is Another who testifies about Me, and I know that the testimony He gives about Me is valid. ³³You have sent messengers to John, and he has testified to the truth. ³⁴I don't receive man's testimony, but I say these things so that you may be saved. ³⁵John was a burning and shining lamp, and for a time you were willing to enjoy his light.

³⁶"But I have a greater testimony than John's because of the works that the Father has given Me to accomplish. These very works I am doing testify about Me that the Father has sent Me. ³⁷The Father who sent Me has Himself testified about Me. You have not heard His voice at any time, and you haven't seen His form. ³⁸You don't have His word living in you, because you don't believe the One He sent. ³⁹You pore over the Scriptures because you think you have eternal life in them, yet they testify about Me. ⁴⁰And you are not willing to come to Me so that you may have life.

⁴¹"I do not accept glory from men, ⁴²but I know you—that you have no love for God within you. ⁴³I have come in My Father's name, yet you don't accept Me. If someone else comes in his own name, you will accept him. ⁴⁴How can you believe? While accepting glory from one another, you don't seek the glory that comes from the only God. ⁴⁵Do not think that I will accuse you to the Father. Your accuser is Moses, on whom you have set your hope. ⁴⁶For if you believed Moses, you would believe Me, because he wrote about Me. ⁴⁷But if you don't believe his writings, how will you believe My words?"

One of the ironies of John's Gospel is the presence of people who demand miracles but are unable to accept them when they occur. This reveals the fundamental necessity of faith, that we must believe before we see, that we must believe in order to see.

Jesus had healed a man who was lame for thirty-eight years, and all the Jews saw was an infraction of one of their rules. This is the context for Jesus' first long discourse in John's Gospel.

Jesus opens in verse 17 by using the word *work* twice, because working on the Sabbath was the central point of contention. The rabbis had conceded that God himself still performed two kinds of work, even on the Sabbath: he judged and he created life. Jesus will echo that he is doing these very same works himself. He is authorized by the Father to judge (v. 22) and he is giving life. The key theme of this long discourse is Jesus' subordination to the Father who sent him. It is the language of the prophet like Moses, who only speaks the words that God gives him to speak. That is the "work" he has been given to do. Alone, he can do nothing (v. 19). Jesus is only doing what he sees the Father doing.

In verse 20, Jesus says the Father loves the Son. In response to all the discussions on the various Greek words for "love" that subordinate the Greek word *phileo* as somehow inferior to the word *agape* (both words are translated "love"), here the word *phileo* is used to describe God's love for Jesus. That can hardly be understood as an inferior form of love.

Verse 24 opens with Jesus' solemn "amen, amen." It is his promise that those who hear and believe his word will become the possessors of eternal life and will not be judged. These are the two works of God that Jesus will begin to carry out, even on the Sabbath. Verse 26 repeats the notion yet again. That a time is coming when life will be given to the dead upon hearing the voice of Jesus, the Son of Man. That same Son of Man who has been given authority to judge (v. 27). Verses 25-27 might seem like a prediction for the distant future. But Jesus clearly said that the time has now come. The dead who hear are standing all around listening to Jesus' word, receiving new life and at that very moment are being rescued from condemnation.

Verses 28-29 take the same pattern of hearing, being raised and saved from condemnation and places it into the future, into a time that is coming. These dead are clearly in their graves. This time of condemnation or being rescued from judgment marks the end of the world and the final day.

In verse 30 Jesus repeats once more that by himself he can do nothing. He has only come to please the One who sent him, to speak his word and to do his work.

The final section of chapter 5 has to do with a lengthy discussion of testimony, of Jesus' testimony about himself and of others testimonies concerning him. He will outline four different kinds of testimony that point to the truth and validity of his ministry and give the reasons for the Jews' disregard of these testimonies.

- Self testimony: according to the Mishnah "none may be believed when he testifies of himself."[2]

- The testimony of John the Baptist: valuable but insufficient because it is human testimony.

- God's work: they don't believe the testimony of God's work because it still requires faith to understand.

- Scripture: they have degraded the Scriptures with their oral law so that the testimony of Scripture is no longer understood.

First, says Jesus, his testimony is not valid. Notice he does not say his testimony is not true, for indeed it is. But according to their "rules made by men" Jesus' testimony is invalid. Next, he points out that they sent investigative committees to John to discover the truth about Jesus. Even though they appeared to align themselves for a time with John ("were willing to enjoy his light"), they ultimately abandoned John when he condemned their hypocrisy (see Mt 3:7).

Finally, that both the word and the work of God is demonstrated in Jesus' life and ministry should convince them of the truth. The work Jesus describes as the "greater testimony" because it testifies that God had sent him. After all, they had just witnessed the healing of the man who had been lame for thirty-eight years. But because of their blindness and stubborn disbelief, they could not accept this weightier testimony, a testimony that is clearly spoken about in the Old Testament (Is 35:6; Jer 31:8).

The irony is not lost on Jesus. He muses that though they pore over the Scriptures because they believe them to be the source of eternal life, yet they refuse to listen to the Scriptures that so clearly speak of him.

Jesus concludes with a contrast between his true motivation and theirs. As always, he asserts he does what he does not to obtain praise for men, which he consistently rejects. They, on the other hand, accept praise from one another. They accept others who come in their own name, but not Jesus, who comes in the name of the Father. The image of

Jesus' words in verses 45-47 comes into sharp focus when we understand that the Pharisees referred to themselves as "disciples of Moses" (see Jn 9:28 NIV). When the time comes, Jesus says, he will not be the one to accuse them before the great assembly. The one who will accuse them for rejecting the flood of testimony concerning Jesus will be Moses himself, the one they set all their hopes on. Jesus concludes, to their horror, that they obviously do not believe Moses, because he has written about Jesus. If they do not truly believe what Moses wrote how will they believe what Jesus says?

JOHN 6

THE TURN TOWARD SCANDAL

¹After this, Jesus crossed the Sea of Galilee (or Tiberias). ²And a huge crowd was following Him because they saw the signs that He was performing by healing the sick. ³So Jesus went up a mountain and sat down there with His disciples.

⁴Now the Passover, a Jewish festival, was near. ⁵Therefore, when Jesus looked up and noticed a huge crowd coming toward Him, He asked Philip, "Where will we buy bread so these people can eat?" ⁶He asked this to test him, for He Himself knew what He was going to do.

⁷Philip answered, "Two hundred denarii worth of bread wouldn't be enough for each of them to have a little."

⁸One of His disciples, Andrew, Simon Peter's brother, said to Him, ⁹"There's a boy here who has five barley loaves and two fish—but what are they for so many?"

¹⁰Then Jesus said, "Have the people sit down."

There was plenty of grass in that place, so they sat down. The men numbered about 5,000. ¹¹Then Jesus took the loaves, and after giving thanks He distributed them to those who were seated—so also with the fish, as much as they wanted.

¹²When they were full, He told His disciples, "Collect the leftovers so that nothing is wasted." ¹³So they collected them and filled 12 baskets with the pieces from the five barley loaves that were left over by those who had eaten.

¹⁴When the people saw the sign He had done, they said, "This really is the Prophet who was to come into the world!" ¹⁵Therefore, when Jesus knew that they were about to come and take Him by force to make Him king, He withdrew again to the mountain by Himself.

Chapter 6 is the hinge on which the story of John's Gospel turns. It marks a radical shift in Jesus' ministry: from his greatest moment of acceptance and popularity to one of the darkest instances of offense and rejection.

The best guess is that approximately six months have passed since the close of chapter 5. Jesus is back in Galilee now and crosses the lake. The

Synoptics picture him constantly crisscrossing the Sea of Galilee, or the sea of Tiberius, the name by which John's readers know the lake. A great crowd follows Jesus, literally thousands of people (v. 10). John is sensitive to the motivation of the crowd. Why are they following Jesus? Because they have witnessed his healing power and have presumably followed him to the other side of the lake hoping to see more miraculous signs. The reminder that Passover is near is ominous in tone. It tells us that Jesus has slightly more than one year left before the final Passover and his cross. This then is the second Passover of Jesus' ministry and the only one Jesus spends in Galilee.

Jesus is sitting, watching the great multitude as they draw near and begin to settle in around him. If we synchronize all the various locations from the other Gospels (this is the only miracle that appears in all four), we can determine that they are close to the city of Bethsaida (see Mt 14:13-21; Mk 6:30-44; Lk 9:10-17). Matthew tells us that evening is approaching. Mark lets us know that Jesus and his disciples have crossed the lake in an attempt to get away from the demands of the crowd (Mk 6:31).

It makes sense that Jesus would first ask Philip where they might purchase bread for the crowd, since he was from Bethsaida and would have local knowledge. It is not hard to imagine a twinkle in Jesus' eye as he asks the question. The issue is really not a matter of where but how in the world could they afford to feed so many. John, conditioned by having told the story a thousand times, whispers to us reassuringly that Jesus already had in mind what he was about to do. That is, he is not just "messing with" Philip.

Philip answers not with a "where" answer but with the far more cogent "how much?" Two hundred denarii, almost a year's wages, would not even put a dent into the bill. The situation is hopeless. What's more to the point, the disciples need to understand just how hopeless it is.

My mentor William Lane used to say that the followers of Jesus should always work at the level of their own inadequacy. We shouldn't be satisfied simply doing the things we are good at. We should strive to be right on the edge so that if the Lord doesn't show up to help us, we will fail miserably. This is the kind of place the disciples are now in.

Just then Andrew, Peter's brother, speaks up. Philip and Andrew seem to be a team (see Jn 1:44; 12:22; Mk 3:18; Acts 1:13). In his naiveté Andrew is trying to fix this unfixable situation. He has found a boy who has five barley loaves and two small fish. Barley was considered food for beasts. Roman soldiers were forced to eat barley bread as part of a severe discipline called decimation. So the bread is crummy and the fish are small, and more than five thousand hungry people are waiting to eat as it is getting dark!

Since it is almost Passover, that means spring and abundant grass. Mark gives the detail that the grass was green. Jesus has the people sit down in orderly groups (see Mk 6:40). In verse 11 you will miss the un-miraculous miracle if you're not paying close attention. All Jesus does is "give thanks." He simply says the blessing. There is not a hint of miraculous language. This has led some scholars to conclude that in fact no miracle occurred. But in verse 14, the people willingly acknowledge that a miraculous sign has occurred. To discount the miraculous nature of this event is to misunderstand the way Jesus performed virtually every miracle. Everyone eats their fill on the green hillside of Galilee. Then Jesus, being very much the rabbi, orders that the leftovers be collected. In Judaism the leftovers were referred to as the *peah* and were always gathered after the meal and given to the slaves.[1] This is where the real miracle behind the miracle occurs.

The key to understanding this miracle is found in the Greek word translated "basket." In the two miraculous feedings—of the four thousand and later of the five thousand—in every account two different words are used to describe the baskets that were used to collect leftovers. Here it is the Greek word *kophinos*, which denotes a small wicker lunch-pail-size basket. The miracle? Exactly twelve small baskets are collected. The point of the miracle is perfect provision for the Twelve disciples, who are now serving as slaves.[2]

Though the miracle was subdued, some of the people recognize it as a sign. Their conclusion is that Jesus is the Prophet. Though they do not speak the full title, the people are referring to the Prophet like Moses. Jesus has provided bread for them in the wilderness, just as Moses had provided the manna (Ex 16:31; Deut 8:16). So profound is their conviction that the crowd is about to take matters into their own hands and force Jesus to be a king. The result of such a large crowd, perhaps as many as twenty thousand, taking such a rebellious action would have ended like so many other rebellions—massive bloodshed and loss of life (see Acts 5:37; 21:38). To save their lives and preserve his life for the time being, Jesus slips away into the hills alone.

THE I AM OF WHO HE IS

16 When evening came, His disciples went down to the sea, 17 got into a boat, and started across the sea to Capernaum. Darkness had already set in, but Jesus had not yet come to them. 18 Then a high wind arose, and the sea began to churn. 19 After they had rowed about three or four miles, they saw Jesus walking on the sea. He was coming near the boat, and they were afraid.

20 But He said to them, "It is I. Don't be afraid!" 21 Then they were willing to take Him on board, and at once the boat was at the shore where they were heading.

22 The next day, the crowd that had stayed on the other side of the sea knew there had been only one boat. They also knew that Jesus had not boarded the boat with His disciples, but that His disciples had gone off alone. 23 Some boats from Tiberias came near the place where they ate the bread after the Lord gave thanks. 24 When the crowd saw that neither Jesus nor His disciples were there, they got into the boats and went to Capernaum looking for Jesus.

Matthew tells us Jesus put the Twelve into a boat and sent them to the other side of the lake before he retreated up into the hills (Mt 14:22). Dark had fallen and the disciples were rowing into a strong, contrary wind. This is not the demonic storm of Matthew 8 and Mark 4, which occurred earlier in the ministry. John has chosen to omit the account of that storm. As they near the halfway point, the disciples look out on the lake and see Jesus walking in their direction. Mark 6:48 gives the interesting detail that Jesus was about to walk past them, which seems even more eerie and terrifying. Walking on the water was a clear indication of Jesus' divinity (Job 9:8-11; Ps 89:9). John omits the detail of the story about Peter, at Jesus' command, walking on the water.

Above the roaring wind they hear a familiar voice. The literal Greek is more succinct, "I am, no fear." Though there is not general agreement on this question, Jesus may be uttering the divine name of God, I Am (Ex 3:14). He is revealing his divinity by walking on the water; perhaps by using the divine name he is expressing his divinity as well.

When Jesus reaches the boat, their fears vanish. He is welcomed on board. Immediately they find themselves on the other side of the lake. It is not clear whether this is an additional facet of the miracle or not.

The next morning the crowd, perhaps still harboring royal ambitions for Jesus, discover that he is gone. They remember that he had not gotten into the boat with his disciples.[3] Climbing into their boats the crowd assumes that Jesus has returned to his home base in Capernaum.

THE BREAD KING

[25]*When they found Him on the other side of the sea, they said to Him, "Rabbi, when did You get here?"*

[26]*Jesus answered, "I assure you: You are looking for Me, not because you saw the signs, but because you ate the loaves and were filled.* [27]*Don't work for the food that perishes but for the food that lasts for eternal life, which the Son of Man will give you, because God the Father has set His seal of approval on Him."*

[28]*"What can we do to perform the works of God?" they asked.*

[29]*Jesus replied, "This is the work of God—that you believe in the One He has sent."*

[30]*"What sign then are You going to do so we may see and believe You?" they asked. "What are You going to perform?* [31]*Our fathers ate the manna in the wilderness, just as it is written: He gave them bread from heaven to eat."*

[32]*Jesus said to them, "I assure you: Moses didn't give you the bread from heaven, but My Father gives you the real bread from heaven.* [33]*For the bread of God is the One who comes down from heaven and gives life to the world."*

[34]*Then they said, "Sir, give us this bread always!"*

[35]*"I am the bread of life," Jesus told them. "No one who comes to Me will ever be hungry, and no one who believes in Me will ever be thirsty again.* [36]*But as I told you, you've seen Me, and yet you do not believe.* [37]*Everyone the Father gives Me will come to Me, and the one who comes to Me I will never*

cast out. ³⁸*For I have come down from heaven, not to do My will, but the will of Him who sent Me. ³⁹This is the will of Him who sent Me: that I should lose none of those He has given Me but should raise them up on the last day. ⁴⁰For this is the will of My Father: that everyone who sees the Son and believes in Him may have eternal life, and I will raise him up on the last day."*

⁴¹*Therefore the Jews started complaining about Him because He said, "I am the bread that came down from heaven." ⁴²They were saying, "Isn't this Jesus the son of Joseph, whose father and mother we know? How can He now say, 'I have come down from heaven'?"*

⁴³*Jesus answered them, "Stop complaining among yourselves. ⁴⁴No one can come to Me unless the Father who sent Me draws him, and I will raise him up on the last day. ⁴⁵It is written in the Prophets: And they will all be taught by God. Everyone who has listened to and learned from the Father comes to Me— ⁴⁶not that anyone has seen the Father except the One who is from God. He has seen the Father.*

⁴⁷*"I assure you: Anyone who believes has eternal life. ⁴⁸I am the bread of life. ⁴⁹Your fathers ate the manna in the wilderness, and they died. ⁵⁰This is the bread that comes down from heaven so that anyone may eat of it and not die. ⁵¹I am the living bread that came down from heaven. If anyone eats of this bread he will live forever. The bread that I will give for the life of the world is My flesh."*

⁵²*At that, the Jews argued among themselves, "How can this man give us His flesh to eat?"*

⁵³*So Jesus said to them, "I assure you: Unless you eat the flesh of the Son of Man and drink His blood, you do not have life in yourselves. ⁵⁴Anyone who eats My flesh and drinks My blood has eternal life, and I will raise him up on the last day, ⁵⁵because My flesh is real food and My blood is real drink. ⁵⁶The one who eats My flesh and drinks My blood lives in Me, and I in him. ⁵⁷Just as the living Father sent Me and I live because of the Father, so the one who feeds on Me will live because of Me. ⁵⁸This is the bread that came down from heaven; it is not like the manna your fathers ate—and they died. The one who eats this bread will live forever."*

⁵⁹*He said these things while teaching in the synagogue in Capernaum.*

⁶⁰*Therefore, when many of His disciples heard this, they said, "This teaching is hard! Who can accept it?"*

⁶¹Jesus, knowing in Himself that His disciples were complaining about this, asked them, "Does this offend you? ⁶²Then what if you were to observe the Son of Man ascending to where He was before? ⁶³The Spirit is the One who gives life. The flesh doesn't help at all. The words that I have spoken to you are spirit and are life. ⁶⁴But there are some among you who don't believe." (For Jesus knew from the beginning those who would not believe and the one who would betray Him.) ⁶⁵He said, "This is why I told you that no one can come to Me unless it is granted to him by the Father."

⁶⁶From that moment many of His disciples turned back and no longer accompanied Him. ⁶⁷Therefore Jesus said to the Twelve, "You don't want to go away too, do you?"

⁶⁸Simon Peter answered, "Lord, who will we go to? You have the words of eternal life. ⁶⁹We have come to believe and know that You are the Holy One of God!"

⁷⁰Jesus replied to them, "Didn't I choose you, the Twelve? Yet one of you is the Devil!" ⁷¹He was referring to Judas, Simon Iscariot's son, one of the Twelve, because he was going to betray Him.

*E*lements of the crowd (it could hardly have been all twenty thousand of them) find Jesus exactly where they assumed he would be, in Capernaum. They ask him how he got there. They know he didn't come by boat. As with so many other questions, Jesus leaves it completely ignored and unanswered. He goes straight to the matter of their motivation. It is not signs they are looking for but another free meal. They must learn to work for eternal food that never spoils, and not for the bread that so quickly becomes stale (Is 55:2). He is readier to give them this eternal bread than he was the barley loaves on the other side of the lake. The reference to the "seal of approval" Jesus says the Father has placed on him might refer to the seal that was placed on offerings by the priests to signify that they were acceptable or approved of for use as a sacrificial offering. If this is what Jesus meant, it is an ominous statement. It means that he will be the living bread that will someday be broken.

The people have missed the deeper significance of what Jesus was saying regarding the eternal bread. They fixate on the word *work*. According to their works-righteousness belief system, they must find and perform the work that God requires.

Jesus speaks into their old orthodoxy the fresh freedom of the new reality. The work is to believe in him. Had they accepted it, it would have opened the door into a new unheard of world. Their misunderstanding will lead to John's central motif by verse 34.

Having just miraculously fed them on the other side of the lake, their request for a miraculous sign in order to believe now rings hollow. It is not really a sign they want, it's another meal (v. 26). Verse 31 is a not so subtle hint. They want what their forefathers ate in the wilderness, manna.

Manna is a fascinating Hebrew word that connects wonderfully to John's motif of misunderstanding. The particle *ma* represents a question mark in Hebrew. The particle *na* is an exclamation point. *Manna* might be literally rendered "? !" It is a reflection on how puzzled the Israelites were when they first saw the mysterious honey-flavored wafers God provided in the wilderness (Ex 16:31). The people come asking for bread not realizing that Jesus is the bread. They ask for a new miracle, not realizing that he is the miracle. He is the true bread from heaven, not the Old Testament manna. Jesus has spoken a deep spiritual truth, and so we can expect the response of the crowd will be misunderstanding. Oblivious to the depth before which they are poised, stubbornly they stick to the request for a free meal, responding, "Give us this bread." They have unknowingly set the scene for the most scandalous of all of Jesus' sayings.

He is the bread he hinted at in verse 33. He will satisfy their hunger forever. The sad truth is, however, that even with all they have seen, they refuse to believe. It is important that we hear Jesus' promise that he will never drive away the ones the Father has given him, because, in a few verses, it will appear that Jesus is doing everything in his power to drive them away! He reiterates that the will of the One who sent him is that he will not lose a single one. Twice he pronounces that he will raise them up on the last day (Jn 6:39-40).

This is all beginning to sound suspect to the people. They begin to "murmur." It is the identical word that is used in the Septuagint, the ancient Greek translation of the Old Testament that Paul used in his writings, to describe how the children of Israel murmured in the wilderness. It is not so much Jesus' reference that he is the bread that bothers them as much as him saying that he had come down from heaven (vv. 41-42, 44).

Jesus responds, telling them to keep their complaining and grumbling to themselves. God will draw them (v. 44) and will teach them (v. 45). Everyone who listens to God will come to Jesus and find everlasting life.

For the second time Jesus proclaims that he is the "bread of life" (v. 48). He explains how the living bread is better than the manna that briefly dealt with the hunger of the people and ultimately still could not keep them from dying in the desert. For the third time Jesus calls himself the "living bread" (or "bread of life") that will satisfy a person's hunger forever. Perhaps some of the people in the crowd were beginning to soften to Jesus' scandalous word. Their brief moment of illusory clarity is about to be shattered. The bread, says Jesus, is his own flesh.

Earlier it was obvious that they wanted more of the bread that Jesus had fed them with the day before. Now the question is, do they want the bread Jesus is now alluding to? The answer is no.

To a group of men and women who scrupulously follow the kosher restrictions of clean and unclean, it sounds as if Jesus has just spoken of cannibalism! It is not too much to assume that some of them may have actually become physically ill when they heard Jesus' words. Two more times he restates the notion of drinking his blood and eating his flesh. For the fourth time he promises to raise them up on the last day. To the 1 percent who were still clinging to the hope that this all is some sort of bizarre metaphor, Jesus makes it clear: his flesh is real food; his blood is real drink. For the fourth time Jesus speaks of eating his flesh and drinking his blood. The repetitions are becoming brutal by this point. He expresses the horrific image of feeding on him. For the second time he reminds his stunned listeners that their forefathers died in the wilderness after eating the earthly manna. The people are shocked, stunned and scandalized. To top it all off, John whispers in our ears that Jesus said all of this in the synagogue in Capernaum. This is most definitely not "synagogue talk."

His disciples respond by objecting that what Jesus is saying is hard to accept. When they ask, "Who can accept it?" the obvious answer is no one.

Again, as in verse 41, the people began to murmur. Having done his best to offend them, both with the scandalous content as well as all of the jackhammer repetitions, Jesus asked, "Does this offend you?"

The word used for "offend" is *scandalizo*, from which we derive our word *scandal*. It is one of the easiest-to-answer questions Jesus ever asked. Like the bread that had "come down" from heaven (vv. 41, 50, 51, 58), so Jesus, the true bread, will someday soon go back up into heaven. And what will they do when they see that miraculous sign?

Verse 63 is as close to an explanation as they will ever receive from Jesus. It is not the flesh that counts but the spirit. He has been speaking spiritual, life-giving words. John whispers that from the beginning Jesus knew who would believe and who would not, who would stay despite his scandalous words and who would go. No one can come unless the Father makes it possible. Given the magnitude of the scandal, who could possibly ever come on their own! Many of his disciples, scandalized and disillusioned, simply walk away. These were not merely members of the crowd but men and women who had made some sort of commitment to Jesus.

Jesus turns back to the Twelve and asks a question that in Greek expects a no answer. It might be translated, "You don't want to leave too, do you?" Peter responds for the others. He is quickly becoming their spokesperson, the one in whom the group is already finding a corporate identity. His tone is one of loyal despair. He is not leaving because there is no place, no one, to whom he can go. Perhaps this is the deepest scandal of all. Through clenched teeth, once again saying more than he knows, Peter affirms Jesus' identity. He is the Holy One of God.

If Jesus were simply trying to drum up as many followers as possible, he might give Peter and the others a glimmer of encouragement in the face of all the scandal they have just endured. Instead, he turns to the issue of one of his followers who will turn out to be a devil. Whispering, John makes it clear that Jesus was referring to Judas (v. 71).

From successful bread king to scandalous lunatic in the span of just one chapter—the tide has begun to turn. In the next verse (Jn 7:1; see also Jn 7:25) we will discover that there are people waiting in Jerusalem to murder Jesus, the misunderstood Messiah.

JOHN 7

"COME TO ME AND DRINK"

7:1–44

FEARSOME FOOLS

7:45-53

"COME TO ME AND DRINK"

¹After this, Jesus traveled in Galilee, since He did not want to travel in Judea because the Jews were trying to kill Him. ²The Jewish Festival of Tabernacles was near, ³so His brothers said to Him, "Leave here and go to Judea so Your disciples can see Your works that You are doing. ⁴For no one does anything in secret while he's seeking public recognition. If You do these things, show Yourself to the world." ⁵(For not even His brothers believed in Him.)

⁶Jesus told them, "My time has not yet arrived, but your time is always at hand. ⁷The world cannot hate you, but it does hate Me because I testify about it—that its deeds are evil. ⁸Go up to the festival yourselves. I'm not going up to the festival yet, because My time has not yet fully come." ⁹After He had said these things, He stayed in Galilee.

¹⁰After His brothers had gone up to the festival, then He also went up, not openly but secretly. ¹¹The Jews were looking for Him at the festival and saying, "Where is He?" ¹²And there was a lot of discussion about Him among the crowds. Some were saying, "He's a good man." Others were saying, "No, on the contrary, He's deceiving the people." ¹³Still, nobody was talking publicly about Him because they feared the Jews.

¹⁴When the festival was already half over, Jesus went up into the temple complex and began to teach. ¹⁵Then the Jews were amazed and said, "How does He know the Scriptures, since He hasn't been trained?"

¹⁶Jesus answered them, "My teaching isn't Mine but is from the One who sent Me. ¹⁷If anyone wants to do His will, he will understand whether the teaching is from God or if I am speaking on My own. ¹⁸The one who speaks for himself seeks his own glory. But He who seeks the glory of the One who sent Him is true, and there is no unrighteousness in Him. ¹⁹Didn't Moses give you the law? Yet none of you keeps the law! Why do you want to kill Me?"

²⁰"You have a demon!" the crowd responded. "Who wants to kill You?"

²¹"I did one work, and you are all amazed," Jesus answered. ²²"Consider this: Moses has given you circumcision—not that it comes from Moses but from the fathers—and you circumcise a man on the Sabbath. ²³If a man receives circumcision on the Sabbath so that the law of Moses won't be broken, are you angry at Me because I made a man entirely well on the Sabbath? ²⁴Stop judging according to outward appearances; rather judge according to righteous judgment."

[25]Some of the people of Jerusalem were saying, "Isn't this the man they want to kill? [26]Yet, look! He's speaking publicly and they're saying nothing to Him. Can it be true that the authorities know He is the Messiah? [27]But we know where this man is from. When the Messiah comes, nobody will know where He is from."

[28]As He was teaching in the temple complex, Jesus cried out, "You know Me and you know where I am from. Yet I have not come on My own, but the One who sent Me is true. You don't know Him; [29]I know Him because I am from Him, and He sent Me."

[30]Then they tried to seize Him. Yet no one laid a hand on Him because His hour had not yet come. [31]However, many from the crowd believed in Him and said, "When the Messiah comes, He won't perform more signs than this man has done, will He?"

[32]The Pharisees heard the crowd muttering these things about Him, so the chief priests and the Pharisees sent temple police to arrest Him.

[33]Then Jesus said, "I am only with you for a short time. Then I'm going to the One who sent Me. [34]You will look for Me, but you will not find Me; and where I am, you cannot come."

[35]Then the Jews said to one another, "Where does He intend to go so we won't find Him? He doesn't intend to go to the Dispersion among the Greeks and teach the Greeks, does He? [36]What is this remark He made: 'You will look for Me, and you will not find Me; and where I am, you cannot come'?"

[37]On the last and most important day of the festival, Jesus stood up and cried out, "If anyone is thirsty, he should come to Me and drink! [38]The one who believes in Me, as the Scripture has said, will have streams of living water flow from deep within him." [39]He said this about the Spirit. Those who believed in Jesus were going to receive the Spirit, for the Spirit had not yet been received because Jesus had not yet been glorified.

[40]When some from the crowd heard these words, they said, "This really is the Prophet!" [41]Others said, "This is the Messiah!" But some said, "Surely the Messiah doesn't come from Galilee, does He? [42]Doesn't the Scripture say that the Messiah comes from David's offspring and from the town of Bethlehem, where David once lived?" [43]So a division occurred among the crowd because of Him. [44]Some of them wanted to seize Him, but no one laid hands on Him.

$\mathcal{A}$fter the turnaround in chapter 6, with some of Jesus' own disciples becoming scandalized by his talk of eating his flesh and drinking his blood, chapter 7 represents an accelerated movement toward the maelstrom. Jesus will be threatened by the people and mocked by his own brothers; the crowds will try to seize him, and fierce temple guards will try in vain to arrest him. In the midst of it all we will witness one of the most dramatic and engaging moments in his ministry.

In light of the scandal that closed the previous chapter, John tells us Jesus confines his movements to the province of Galilee, staying away from Judea to the south. This hints at the fact that the two regions were radically different. Galilee was home, with its relatively lax observance of the oral traditions, with its simpler rural population. Judea was more metro-polite. Observance of the oral tradition was far stricter. Judea was not a safe place for Jesus to linger. There were people waiting there to kill him, which a year from now they will do.

It is fall, our month of September, the season of Tabernacles or Succoth. Tabernacles has two facets, one historical, the other agricultural. Historically the children of Israel lived in succoth or booths when they were wandering in the wilderness. Succoth was a festival designed to help the people remember the wilderness wanderings. Its agricultural significance, coming at the season of harvest, celebrates the ingathering, the season when harvesters live in the fields in small huts, also known as succoth.

In verse 3 we have our only glimpse into Jesus' relationship with his brothers. Matthew provides a list of their names; James, Joseph, Simon and Judas (or Jude, as he is more commonly known). James and Jude will become believers after the resurrection. But for now, they are antagonists, mocking the fact that Jesus is "acting in secret."

Derisively they say that Jesus should do his miracles in public if he wants to become a public figure. John whispers their mindset: even they did not believe (v. 5). If Jesus had wanted to be a public figure, to attract a large group of followers, he would have hardly spoken those scandalous words about eating his flesh and drinking his blood in chapter 6. Jesus responds that they can come and go as they like. Things are different for Jesus, who in obedience to the One who sent him is walking the narrow path of radical obedience. They leave. He stays in Galilee for the time being.

The picture of the hiding Jesus is not a popular image, yet the Gospels show him trying to hide more than once (Mt 14:13; Mk 7:24; Jn 7:1; 8:59; 11:54; 12:36). Jesus secretly makes his way to Jerusalem amidst a crowd that is wondering where he might be and when he might turn up. Note that they are whispering because they are afraid of the "Jews," that is, the scribes and Pharisees. In chapter 9 we will discover that a formal ban has been issued concerning Jesus and anyone who associates with him.

In verse 14 Jesus begins a public teaching appearance in the temple court. His teaching style does not reflect any academic background; that is, he never quotes any other sources. In verses 16-19 he seems to be summing up a lesson that John has omitted. His teaching does not come from great contemporary teachers like either Hillel or Shammai, but straight from God himself. It is unique and authoritative. In verse 18 we can detect a shadow of his brothers' mockery. He is not speaking to gain honor for himself. Once again the scandalous discourse in chapter 6 was hardly the sort of speech that gains public honor. They have the law, given to them by Moses, but none of them keeps the law. In verse 1 John mentioned that people there were waiting there to kill Jesus. Now he makes reference to them once more. Not for the first time, the crowd accuses Jesus of being demon possessed (v. 20). They are shocked at his reference that someone is trying to kill him. What sort of delusion is he under? When Jesus says in verse 21 that they are "amazed" because of one of his miracles, we need to understand that their astonishment has nothing to do with a miracle but the fact that Jesus had violated the Sabbath (Jn 5:1-15). Jesus observes that they circumcise infants on the Sabbath. (If the eighth day after the birth was a Sabbath, a child was still circumcised.) If they can wound on the Sabbath, why can't Jesus heal?

Earlier they derided Jesus, saying, "Who wants to kill you?" (v. 20). Now in verse 25 the confusion of the crowd is compounded. "Isn't this the man they want to kill?" some of them say. He is speaking publicly, something he had avoided during the time he was staying safe in Galilee. Why isn't anyone doing anything about it? In verse 30 some of them will take matters into their own hands when they try to seize Jesus, who accused them of not knowing God (v. 28).

Jesus escapes the tumult of the mob. John gives us no explanation aside from the statement that his "time" had not yet come. Each time this phrase is spoken in John it reminds us that a time is coming for Jesus (see Jn 12:23). It is a divided and confused crowd that Jesus leaves behind. Some believe; others no doubt are frustrated at their missed opportunity to kill him. This element of the crowd, the chief priests and the Pharisees, hearing what people are whispering about Jesus, send a detachment of fierce temple guards to arrest Jesus. This police force was chosen exclusively from the tribe of Benjamin, which was known as the bravest of the twelve tribes. The battle cry of Israel was "After thee, O Benjamin!" (Hos 5:8 KJV).

In some secluded corner, Jesus warns that he will only be with them for a short time. He will soon return to the One who sent him. Even though they try to find him, they will not be able to do so (see Prov 1:28; Is 55:6). It was a deeply spiritual statement, and so we should expect a misunderstanding. This is precisely what happens in verses 35-36. In trying to guess where Jesus might be going, the crowd wonders if he intends to go and teach among the Greeks, that is, among the Jewish communities scattered throughout the Hellenistic world.

A few days later, on the final day of the feast, Jesus shouts from the middle of the crowd what he had earlier calmly proposed to the Samaritan woman at the well. If they will come to him, he will give them living water, that is the Spirit. (See the introduction for the treatment of this passage.) This is one of the most dramatic moments in Jesus' ministry. It ties together Jesus' courage, the scandal and his radical obedience to the Father. Never forget that as he speaks these luminous words, the crowd surrounding him is peppered with men who are waiting for the opportunity to kill him. In the midst of the spiritual drought that was the temple, in the shadow of death Jesus is shouting words of life and offering them living water.

Don't forget that this occurs during Tabernacles, a festival that celebrates the wandering of the children of Israel in the wilderness. There, in the wilderness, Moses struck the rock and provided water (Ex 17:1-7).

In this context, as Jesus promises once more to provide living water, Jesus sounds to the people like another Moses figure, the Prophet like Moses (v. 40). (Note Jesus will never call himself the water; this is a symbol reserved for the Holy Spirit.)

The scene dissolves into confusion. Some say he is the Prophet, some say he is the Christ, others argue about where he was from. The Messiah does not come from Galilee, and yet Jesus is known to be from there. Apparently they don't know the detail that Jesus was actually born in Bethlehem. The total tonnage of what they do not understand would sink a ship. Those who had been sent to seize him dearly wanted to do so, yet no one was able to summon the courage to do it. Jesus appears to be the only courageous person in Jerusalem. One of Hillel's favorite sayings was, "In a place where there are no men, try to be a man."[1] Jesus would have been aware of this saying.

FEARSOME FOOLS

[45]*Then the temple police came to the chief priests and Pharisees, who asked them, "Why haven't you brought Him?"*

[46]*The police answered, "No man ever spoke like this!"*

[47]*Then the Pharisees responded to them: "Are you fooled too?* [48]*Have any of the rulers or Pharisees believed in Him?* [49]*But this crowd, which doesn't know the law, is accursed!"*

[50]*Nicodemus—the one who came to Him previously, being one of them— said to them,* [51]*"Our law doesn't judge a man before it hears from him and knows what he's doing, does it?"*

[52]*"You aren't from Galilee too, are you?" they replied. "Investigate and you will see that no prophet arises from Galilee."*

[53]*So each one went to his house.*

*T*he guards who were sent in verse 32 now return empty-handed. They have disobeyed a direct order from the most powerful man in Israel, the high priest. The fierce warriors can only mutter, "No man ever spoke the way he does."

The Pharisees explode. Have they been deceived like the fools who were a moment ago whispering that Jesus might be the Christ? When they upbraid the guards, saying that none of the Pharisees have been deceived, they show that they are unaware that two of their party, Joseph and Nicodemus, are already secret followers of Jesus. In fact, at this moment Nicodemus interrupts their venomous monologue with a point of law. No one could be condemned without a hearing (Ex 23:1; Deut 1:16).

Imagine the tense moment when they snap at Nicodemus, "Are you from Galilee too?" That is, are you a follower and obviously on Jesus' side? They try to win the moment by insinuating that Nicodemus needs to go back and read his Bible. Doesn't he know that a prophet, and certainly not *the* Prophet, does not come from Galilee? The fact is Jonah was from Galilee. Whether Nicodemus knows this or not, and I suspect he does, for now he keeps his mouth shut.

JOHN 8

A PROBLEM PASSAGE

8:1–11

FOUR PRECIOUS PROMISES

8:12–59

A PROBLEM PASSAGE

¹But Jesus went to the Mount of Olives.

²At dawn He went to the temple complex again, and all the people were coming to Him. He sat down and began to teach them.

³Then the scribes and the Pharisees brought a woman caught in adultery, making her stand in the center. ⁴"Teacher," they said to Him, "this woman was caught in the act of committing adultery. ⁵In the law Moses commanded us to stone such women. So what do You say?" ⁶They asked this to trap Him, in order that they might have evidence to accuse Him.

Jesus stooped down and started writing on the ground with His finger. ⁷When they persisted in questioning Him, He stood up and said to them, "The one without sin among you should be the first to throw a stone at her."

⁸Then He stooped down again and continued writing on the ground. ⁹When they heard this, they left one by one, starting with the older men. Only He was left, with the woman in the center. ¹⁰When Jesus stood up, He said to her, "Woman, where are they? Has no one condemned you?"

¹¹"No one, Lord," she answered.

"Neither do I condemn you," said Jesus. "Go, and from now on do not sin anymore."

The story of the woman taken in adultery is one of the most problematic passages in the New Testament in terms of authenticity. Against its genuineness are the facts that the oldest manuscripts of John do not contain it, and none of the church fathers referred to it, showing that their manuscripts did not contain the passage either. In a few manuscripts the passage is found in the Gospel of Luke during the Passion Week narrative. (Scholars refer to this as a "textual floater.") The word *scribe* appears for the only time in John's Gospel here, which may point to a different author. Finally, some believe it interrupts the flow of the narrative.

The most widely held explanation to these problems is that the story was cut from the earliest copies of John because Jesus seems to be condoning adultery. Later it was restored, though its original position in the text had been lost. For a long time this explanation seemed credible to me, but the more I look at the evidence it seems inadequate in explaining all of the problems.

Though it is less strong, a case can also be made for the passage's authenticity. First, its very uniqueness points to John. There is not a hint of the story in any of the Synoptics. The reference to Moses in verse 5 is consistent with John's focus on Moses, who mentions him thirteen times in the Gospel. Verse 6 may be another example of John's habit of speaking parenthetically, of "whispering" a background explanation. Finally the notion of Jesus not coming to condemn or judge appears in other places in John's Gospel (Jn 8:15; 12:47). This story may be John's parabolic representation of the truth, although it is not tied to one of the "I am" sayings. Finally, at the conclusion of the chapter the people will try to do to Jesus what they wanted to do to the woman, that is, to stone him (v. 59).

With all of this evidence on the table, the Jesus of this story is the Jesus of John. (I realize that is a very subjective statement.) He is demonstrating the same over-the-top sort of forgiveness connected with *hesed*. He is infuriating to the Pharisees. Perhaps most of all, Jesus does what he does on so many other occasions; he answers an unanswerable trick question with an unanswerable question of his own.

The scene is set in verse 2. It is early in the morning and the people have already gathered around Jesus in the temple court. If the story is where it belongs in the text, it is still the Feast of Tabernacles.

It is clearly a trap. The Pharisees bring in a woman who they say was caught in the act of adultery. The fact that the man is not brought in as well also points to a setup. Moses commanded to stone such women, the Pharisees say. Actually the passage in Leviticus does not specify how someone is to be executed (Lev 20:10). In verse 6 we hear the very Johannine whisper, "It was a trap." They are looking for something to accuse Jesus of. Like all their trick questions, either response from Jesus will get him into trouble. If he says they should execute her, he will be violating Roman law. The power of life and death had been taken away from the Jews by the Romans except for the ability to execute a Gentile found in the inner courts of the temple. If Jesus says she should not be stoned, he is breaking the law of Moses.

His response rings true to what we would expect from Jesus. It is creative and irritating. He is not "scribbling." The Greek word indicates that he is literally "writing down" something (*kategraphen*). There are multiple guesses in the commentaries as to what Jesus might have been writing in the dust. Some say he is writing down the names of men in the crowd who had also committed adultery. This idea comes from Jeremiah 17:13, which says that all those who turn away from God will have their names written in the dust. The same passage goes on to say that this is because they have forsaken the spring of living water. This provides a wonderful connection back to John 7:37 and Jesus' promise of living water. One ancient variant reading says he was writing down a list of sins, and the onlookers were seeing in the sand the sins they were guilty of.

A newer idea is that Jesus is acting as a Roman judge, who always wrote down a sentence in court before pronouncing it. But this seems somewhat of a stretch to imply that Jesus would copy the actions of one of the Roman authorities. The final answer to the unanswerable question of what Jesus wrote in the sand is that no one knows. Apparently John, if indeed he is the author, does not think we need to know.

The Pharisees are furious at Jesus' curious nonresponse and keep pushing for an answer. When it comes, it is so uniquely luminous that it could have only come from Jesus. If anyone is without sin, then by all means let him cast the first stone. His statement is an echo of Proverbs 20:9: "Who can say, 'I have kept my heart pure, I am cleansed from my sin'?" This connection to the Wisdom writings is another point in favor of the passage being Johannine.

Once more Jesus begins writing in the sand, giving the crowd some silent space to decide what to do. It was a risky move. But it is a move that pays off. Feeling convicted, the older Pharisees leave first. Just why John gives us this detail is also a mystery. Finally everyone has left except Jesus, who is still writing, and the woman. We have not heard a word from her lips until this moment. She has not protested her innocence nor has she pleaded for mercy. Jesus refers to her simply as "woman," the same way he addressed his own mother in chapter 2. He looks around at the empty space and asks, "Has no one condemned you?"

"No one, sir," she replies.

Jesus' final words to her are his words to us as we stand condemned and guilty before him. He has not come to judge but to save. He has absorbed the punishment for our sins as surely as he would've stood between the woman that morning and any stone that might have been thrown at her.

FOUR PRECIOUS PROMISES

[12] Then Jesus spoke to them again: "I am the light of the world. Anyone who follows Me will never walk in the darkness but will have the light of life."

[13] So the Pharisees said to Him, "You are testifying about Yourself. Your testimony is not valid."

[14] "Even if I testify about Myself," Jesus replied, "My testimony is valid, because I know where I came from and where I'm going. But you don't know where I come from or where I'm going. [15] You judge by human standards. I judge no one. [16] And if I do judge, My judgment is true, because I am not alone, but I and the Father who sent Me judge together. [17] Even in your law it is written that the witness of two men is valid. [18] I am the One who testifies about Myself, and the Father who sent Me testifies about Me."

[19] Then they asked Him, "Where is Your Father?"

"You know neither Me nor My Father," Jesus answered. "If you knew Me, you would also know My Father." [20] He spoke these words by the treasury, while teaching in the temple complex. But no one seized Him, because His hour had not come.

[21] Then He said to them again, "I'm going away; you will look for Me, and you will die in your sin. Where I'm going, you cannot come."

[22] So the Jews said again, "He won't kill Himself, will He, since He says, 'Where I'm going, you cannot come'?"

[23] "You are from below," He told them, "I am from above. You are of this world; I am not of this world. [24] Therefore I told you that you will die in your sins. For if you do not believe that I am He, you will die in your sins."

[25] "Who are You?" they questioned.

"Precisely what I've been telling you from the very beginning," Jesus told them. [26] "I have many things to say and to judge about you, but the One who sent Me is true, and what I have heard from Him—these things I tell the world."

²⁷They did not know He was speaking to them about the Father. ²⁸So Jesus said to them, "When you lift up the Son of Man, then you will know that I am He, and that I do nothing on My own. But just as the Father taught Me, I say these things. ²⁹The One who sent Me is with Me. He has not left Me alone, because I always do what pleases Him."

³⁰As He was saying these things, many believed in Him. ³¹So Jesus said to the Jews who had believed Him, "If you continue in My word, you really are My disciples. ³²You will know the truth, and the truth will set you free."

³³"We are descendants of Abraham," they answered Him, "and we have never been enslaved to anyone. How can You say, 'You will become free'?"

³⁴Jesus responded, "I assure you: Everyone who commits sin is a slave of sin. ³⁵A slave does not remain in the household forever, but a son does remain forever. ³⁶Therefore, if the Son sets you free, you really will be free. ³⁷I know you are descendants of Abraham, but you are trying to kill Me because My word is not welcome among you. ³⁸I speak what I have seen in the presence of the Father; therefore, you do what you have heard from your father."

³⁹"Our father is Abraham!" they replied.

"If you were Abraham's children," Jesus told them, "you would do what Abraham did. ⁴⁰But now you are trying to kill Me, a man who has told you the truth that I heard from God. Abraham did not do this! ⁴¹You're doing what your father does."

"We weren't born of sexual immorality," they said. "We have one Father—God."

⁴²Jesus said to them, "If God were your Father, you would love Me, because I came from God and I am here. For I didn't come on My own, but He sent Me. ⁴³Why don't you understand what I say? Because you cannot listen to My word. ⁴⁴You are of your father the Devil, and you want to carry out your father's desires. He was a murderer from the beginning and has not stood in the truth, because there is no truth in him. When he tells a lie, he speaks from his own nature, because he is a liar and the father of liars. ⁴⁵Yet because I tell the truth, you do not believe Me. ⁴⁶Who among you can convict Me of sin? If I tell the truth, why don't you believe Me? ⁴⁷The one who is from God listens to God's words. This is why you don't listen, because you are not from God."

⁴⁸The Jews responded to Him, "Aren't we right in saying that You're a Samaritan and have a demon?"

⁴⁹"I do not have a demon," Jesus answered. "On the contrary, I honor My Father and you dishonor Me. ⁵⁰I do not seek My glory; the One who seeks it also judges. ⁵¹I assure you: If anyone keeps My word, he will never see death—ever!"

⁵²Then the Jews said, "Now we know You have a demon. Abraham died and so did the prophets. You say, 'If anyone keeps My word, he will never taste death—ever!' ⁵³Are You greater than our father Abraham who died? Even the prophets died. Who do You pretend to be?"

⁵⁴"If I glorify Myself," Jesus answered, "My glory is nothing. My Father— you say about Him, 'He is our God'—He is the One who glorifies Me. ⁵⁵You've never known Him, but I know Him. If I were to say I don't know Him, I would be a liar like you. But I do know Him, and I keep His word. ⁵⁶Your father Abraham was overjoyed that he would see My day; he saw it and rejoiced."

⁵⁷The Jews replied, "You aren't 50 years old yet, and You've seen Abraham?"

⁵⁸Jesus said to them, "I assure you: Before Abraham was, I am."

⁵⁹At that, they picked up stones to throw at Him. But Jesus was hidden, and went out of the temple complex.

*T*he remainder of chapter 8 is a continued discussion of the nature of Jesus' deity, his relationship to the Father as well as four fundamental promises he will make to his followers. It is difficult to determine when the discourse takes place. The references to the light may indicate that it is still Tabernacles and Jesus is still in Jerusalem. On the last day of Tabernacles (see Jn 7:37) the illumination of the temple was celebrated. The Torah scrolls were removed and replaced with a candlestick in an allusion to Proverbs 6:23, Psalms 119:105 and Isaiah 60:1. This prayer would be offered on the occasion: "Oh Lord of the universe, thou commanded us to light the lamps to Thee, yet Thou art the Light of the world."

Jesus could be connecting to this image as he had connected to the image of the water in John 7:37. Since *light* was another name for the Messiah (Is 9:1-2; 42:6; 49:6; Mal 4:2), perhaps all these images are coming together in this passage; the historical perspective from Exodus 17 as well as the various passages from the prophets.

Another uniqueness of John's Gospel is his portrayal of the parabolic nature of Jesus' life. One of his most significant omissions are the parables of Jesus. However, John always provides a significant substitution whenever he omits material, and in this case it is the presentation of the life of Jesus as a parable. The first instance was in chapter 6, where Jesus fed the five thousand and later made the pronouncement that he was the bread of life (Jn 6:1-15, 35). Here, perhaps connected to the image of the illumination of the temple, Jesus makes the pronouncement first in verse 12 that he is the light of the world. Later, in chapter 9, in the parable that is his life, Jesus will demonstrate the truth of this pronouncement by opening the eyes of the man born blind. He will deliberately repeat the pronouncement in John 9:5 that he is the light.

The statement that he is the light is tied to a promise in John 8:12. It is a logical conclusion that if indeed he is the light, then those who follow him will walk within the illumination of that light. They will never walk in darkness. It is the first of four significant promises he will make in this chapter.

With verse 13 we plunge back into the argument about the validity of testimony we last heard in chapter 5. Jesus responds that contrary to legal precept his testimony is valid because he knows where he came from and where he is going. The unspoken place of origin and his ultimate destination is heaven. Perhaps referring back to the woman taken in adultery, Jesus reminds them that he judges no one. (Another small hint that the story belongs in John.) But if he judges, his judgment will be true because of his relationship with the Father, the One who sent him. His testimony is valid because it is based on his witness and that of the Father.

Jesus has consistently referred to his Father throughout John's Gospel. In John 5:18 the Jews wanted to kill Jesus for stating that God is his Father. It's hard not to believe that as they asked the question here, "Where is your father?" some of them are bracing themselves for the answer "heaven."

The situation might have gone either way. Jesus chooses not to light the fuse for the time being. He cuts them off saying they do not know either him or the Father.

The eyewitness detail, that this all happened near the place where the offerings were put in, maybe another connection to the event of Tabernacles since there were four large candelabra in the same location that were lighted during the Feast of Tabernacles.

John fails once more to explain how Jesus got away. Did he stare them down? Was he forced to physically resist their grasp? The only explanation is that "his time had not yet come." A time is coming for Jesus and it is less than a year away. We are not told where the remainder of the discussion in chapter 8 takes place. Verse 59 allows us to at least know it was somewhere on the "temple complex."

Connected to his previous statement concerning where he was from and where he was going (v. 14), Jesus reiterates that he is leaving, that they will look for him and will die in their sin. Here Jesus is speaking the words of Ezekiel 3:18. He is fulfilling the prophetic mandate to warn the people concerning their sin (see Jn 7:7). By verse 30 we will see that a few of these listeners begin to put their faith in Jesus.

In response to his statement that they cannot follow where he is going, the Jews make an extraordinary statement. "Will he kill himself?" they ask. It is remarkable to think that at one point in his ministry people entertained the thought that Jesus might be a victim of suicide. This is John's motif of misunderstanding. Jesus has made a deeply spiritual statement concerning his eventual ascension to heaven and return to the One who sent him. The people do not just mildly misunderstand; they grossly misinterpret Jesus' words. The motif functions to set Jesus apart as the story unfolds. He will be lonelier and lonelier until eventually, on the cross, he will be completely alone.

In verses 23-24 Jesus is not speaking condemnation but rather is speaking as the light. If they do not believe, they will die in their sins. The Pharisees seem to be absent at this point. This appears to be a group of people who are moving slowly toward belief in Jesus. Had the Pharisees been there they would have responded to Jesus' words about dying in their sins with explosive, confrontative language. The prospective believers ask the fundamental question, the question that must be answered before anyone can come to Jesus—"Who are you?"

I am told by translators that the second part of verse 25 is the most difficult phrase in the New Testament to translate. A comparison of various translations reveals this:

- "Even that which I have also spoken unto you from the beginning" (ASV)
- "Just what I have been telling you from the beginning" (NIV)
- "Precisely what I've been telling you from the very beginning" (HCSB)
- "The one I have always claimed to be" (NLT)
- "The beginning, who also speak unto you" (DRB)
- "I am who I said I was from the beginning" (GWT)
- "What have I been saying to you *from* the beginning?" (NASB)
- "Even the very same thing that I say unto you" (TNT)

Taken in context, HCSB and NIV seem to be the safest choice. Jesus has openly been confessing who he is from the beginning. He returns to one of the central passages from which he derives his own self-understanding, Deuteronomy 18. Like Moses, Jesus is telling the world what he has heard from the One who sent him.

Consistently Jesus is misunderstood—the more central and significant the truth, the greater the misunderstanding. In verse 27 John whispers that the crowd did not understand that Jesus was telling them about the Father. At this moment, with prospective followers in confusion, we might expect Jesus to back off and perhaps provide a simplifying, didactic explanation. He never does this, apart from explaining the seed parables in private to the Twelve (Mk 4:10, 33). He is not trying to be obtuse or obscure. Jesus understands that belief based on exhaustive explanation is as thin a belief as that based on signs. Coming to faith in him is not based on accepting logical propositions; it is much deeper and mysterious than that. It involves the Father and the Spirit speaking to the heart and mind through the imagination (Jn 3:8; 6:44).

At this point, though we may think we need further explanation, Jesus speaks the perfect words, and they involve the cross. "Lifted up" is a consistent metaphor for crucifixion in John's Gospel (Jn 3:14; 8:28;

12:32, 34). When he is crucified they will know who he is. They will realize that all he said about his relationship to the One who sent him was
true after all. The Father taught him, sent him and has not left him
alone. As the crowd hears Jesus' perfect words, many come to faith without explanation and without seeing a single sign!

To the tiny clutch of newborn followers Jesus gives the second significant promise. If they hold to his teaching, they will know the truth
and the truth will set them free (v. 32). This is not truth as an abstract
philosophical proposition, rather the truth of who Jesus is and what he
means, the truth incarnate. Jesus has spoken a deeply spiritual promise
once more, so what should we expect but misunderstanding.

Josephus said that the Jews have an "inviolable attachment to liberty."[1]
Notice that Jesus did not even insinuate they were slaves. He simply
promised them freedom. Yet the people snap back that because they are
the descendents of Abraham they have never been slaves to anyone.

Jesus responds with a concept that became central to Paul's
thought: sin is something to which all are in slavery until Christ sets
us free to become his slaves (1 Cor 7:21; 9:19; Gal 1:10). Jesus tells
them that, in fact, they are not free despite being Abraham's descendents (who were actually slaves in Egypt). They are in slavery to sin,
from which Jesus has promised to set them free. Jesus, the Son, has
promised to set them free; that means true freedom. Though they are
descendents of Abraham, they have contemplated killing Jesus, who
is telling them only what he heard from the Father. They are obviously listening to their father, says Jesus. Earlier, he had chosen not to
light the fuse in the midst of a heated confrontation with the Pharisees in the temple (v. 19). At that moment the issue was also associated with the question about Jesus' Father. Here, they are confronted
once again with the question of the identity of the Father. Jesus cannot restrain himself any longer. He has pulled the ladder out from
under them already, denying their freedom status. Now he will annul
their descent from Abraham.

They are doing what they heard from their father. They are determined to kill Jesus. This reveals who their father truly is. You can sense
the heat rising when in verse 41 the Jews insinuate that Jesus is illegiti-

mate. Perhaps this is a slap in his face given the miraculous nature of his birth. They insist that God is their father.

Their treatment of Jesus reveals that this could not be true, otherwise, they would love him. Once more Jesus speaks of his identity as the sent One (v. 42). He concludes that they cannot comprehend what he is saying because they belong to a different father, the devil.

Verse 44 provides Jesus' basic understanding of who the devil is. He is first and foremost a murderer. Second, he is a liar. Because Jesus is speaking the language of truth, they cannot understand because the natural language of the devil's children is lies. They are determined to kill him because the devil's children have descended from the original murder (see Rom 5:14).

Verse 46 comes like a bolt out of the blue. Jesus is concluding his argument. They cannot disregard what he has said because of his sinless life, yet they stubbornly disbelieve. Those who hear God belong to him. In John 7:7 Jesus had told his disbelieving brothers that he would show that the world was evil. Here he has done just that.

For the remainder of the chapter the heated words will fire back and forth as Jesus faithfully does the work of the One who sent him by courageously exposing the stubborn sin and disbelief of the crowd.

The opening volley from the crowd consists of name calling. Jesus, they say, is a Samaritan (a synonym for "heretic") and is possessed by a demon. According to Mark 3:28-30 they have just committed the unpardonable sin, attributing the work of Jesus to demons.

Jesus fires back, denying their charge of demon possession, by which they are dishonoring him. He is honoring the Father, seeking his glory, telling his truth. Jesus pours more fuel on the fire with the words of the final promise. Those who keep his word will never see death. This is not the first time he has made this promise (Jn 6:40, 50, 51, 54). He will explain this promise to Martha in John 11:25.

Jesus' remarkable promise only fans the flames. The crowd repeats the charge of demon possession. They reason that Abraham and the prophets all died. Jesus is clearly claiming to be something more than them. He responds that he is not trying to glorify himself. If that were true, it would all be meaningless. It is the Father who is glorifying him, the

Father he so intimately knows and whose word he perfectly keeps. The truth is, Abraham, their father, joyfully looked forward to seeing Jesus' day, and when he saw it, he was glad.

Again and again the characters in the Old Testament were confronted by an individual simply referred to as the "Angel of the Lord." When this angel appears he speaks in first person for God. Many have understood the Angel of the Lord as a Christophany, that is, a pre-incarnate appearance of Jesus:

- In Genesis 16 this Angel shows Hagar a spring of living water that saves her life and that of her infant son. She concludes in verse 13, "You are the God who sees me . . . I have now seen the One who sees me." (NIV)

- In Genesis 22 this same Angel of the Lord says to Abraham, "You have not withheld your only son from Me."

- In Genesis 32:30, after Jacob wrestles with the Angel of the Lord he exclaims, "I saw God face to face, and yet my life was spared." (NIV)

- In Exodus 3:2 the Angel of the Lord appears in the flame of the burning bush. The voice from the bush says in verse 6, "I am the God of your father." In verse 14 the voice says, "I AM WHO I AM."

- In Judges 13, the Angel of the Lord appears to Manoah, the father of Samson. Afterward Manoah exclaims to his wife, "We are doomed to die. . . . We have seen God!" Not only Abraham but Jacob, Hager, Moses and Manoah all saw Jesus' "day"; that is, they all met him through the person referred to as the Angel of the Lord.

A spiritual pronouncement and misunderstanding: the crowd observes that Jesus is not even fifty years old, hardly old enough to have known Abraham. The obtuseness of their response echoes Nicodemus, "How can a man enter his mother's womb?" and the woman at the well, "You have no bucket."

"Amen, amen," Jesus concludes, "before Abraham was, I am" (v. 58).

It is not always clear when Jesus says "I am" whether he has actually spoken the name of God, a name that was not supposed to be pronounced. But here it is obvious. The crowd responds just as Leviticus

24:16 says they should: they pick up stones to stone him.

Once more we see the hiding Jesus. Though it is not said, the inference is clear, his time had not yet come.

Jesus spoke four significant promises in John 8:

- The one who follows him will never walk in darkness. (v. 12)
- The truth will set them free. (v. 32)
- They will be truly free. (v. 36)
- They will never see death. (v. 51)

Jesus promises light, freedom and eternal life. The crowd responds with accusations of demon possession and the threat of death. I hope and believe and trust that a few of those who put their faith in him (v. 30) were able to withstand the scandal.

JOHN 9

"YOU'RE SEEING HIM"

9:1–41

"YOU'RE SEEING HIM"

[1]As He was passing by, He saw a man blind from birth. [2]His disciples questioned Him: "Rabbi, who sinned, this man or his parents, that he was born blind?"

[3]"Neither this man nor his parents sinned," Jesus answered. "This came about so that God's works might be displayed in him. [4]We must do the works of Him who sent Me while it is day. Night is coming when no one can work. [5]As long as I am in the world, I am the light of the world."

[6]After He said these things He spit on the ground, made some mud from the saliva, and spread the mud on his eyes. [7]"Go," He told him, "wash in the pool of Siloam" (which means "Sent"). So he left, washed, and came back seeing.

[8]His neighbors and those who formerly had seen him as a beggar said, "Isn't this the man who sat begging?" [9]Some said, "He's the one." "No," others were saying, "but he looks like him."

He kept saying, "I'm the one!"

[10]Therefore they asked him, "Then how were your eyes opened?"

[11]He answered, "The man called Jesus made mud, spread it on my eyes, and told me, 'Go to Siloam and wash.' So when I went and washed I received my sight."

[12]"Where is He?" they asked.

"I don't know," he said.

[13]They brought the man who used to be blind to the Pharisees. [14]The day that Jesus made the mud and opened his eyes was a Sabbath. [15]So again the Pharisees asked him how he received his sight.

"He put mud on my eyes," he told them. "I washed and I can see."

[16]Therefore some of the Pharisees said, "This man is not from God, for He doesn't keep the Sabbath!" But others were saying, "How can a sinful man perform such signs?" And there was a division among them.

[17]Again they asked the blind man, "What do you say about Him, since He opened your eyes?"

"He's a prophet," he said.

[18]The Jews did not believe this about him—that he was blind and received sight—until they summoned the parents of the one who had received his sight.

[19]They asked them, "Is this your son, the one you say was born blind? How then does he now see?"

20"We know this is our son and that he was born blind," his parents answered. 21"But we don't know how he now sees, and we don't know who opened his eyes. Ask him; he's of age. He will speak for himself." 22His parents said these things because they were afraid of the Jews, since the Jews had already agreed that if anyone confessed Him as Messiah, he would be banned from the synagogue. 23This is why his parents said, "He's of age; ask him."

24So a second time they summoned the man who had been blind and told him, "Give glory to God. We know that this man is a sinner!"

25He answered, "Whether or not He's a sinner, I don't know. One thing I do know: I was blind, and now I can see!"

26Then they asked him, "What did He do to you? How did He open your eyes?"

27"I already told you," he said, "and you didn't listen. Why do you want to hear it again? You don't want to become His disciples too, do you?"

28They ridiculed him: "You're that man's disciple, but we're Moses' disciples. 29We know that God has spoken to Moses. But this man—we don't know where He's from!"

30"This is an amazing thing," the man told them. "You don't know where He is from, yet He opened my eyes! 31We know that God doesn't listen to sinners, but if anyone is God-fearing and does His will, He listens to him. 32Throughout history no one has ever heard of someone opening the eyes of a person born blind. 33If this man were not from God, He wouldn't be able to do anything."

34"You were born entirely in sin," they replied, "and are you trying to teach us?" Then they threw him out.

35When Jesus heard that they had thrown the man out, He found him and asked, "Do you believe in the Son of Man?"

36"Who is He, Sir, that I may believe in Him?" he asked.

37Jesus answered, "You have seen Him; in fact, He is the One speaking with you."

38"I believe, Lord!" he said, and he worshiped Him.

39Jesus said, "I came into this world for judgment, in order that those who do not see will see and those who do see will become blind."

40Some of the Pharisees who were with Him heard these things and asked Him, "We aren't blind too, are we?"

⁴¹*"If you were blind,"* Jesus told them, *"you wouldn't have sin. But now that you say, 'We see'—your sin remains."*

*T*he story of the healing of the man born blind is the best example of John's tendency to focus at length on Jesus' interaction with a solitary individual. The entire chapter is dedicated to the story of a nameless man. It is the only example of Jesus healing someone stricken from birth, and it provides an excellent backdrop for the longstanding discussion concerning the connection between sickness and sin.

We were prepared for the story in John 8:12 when Jesus claimed to be the light of the world. In the parable that is Jesus' life, that statement will now be lived out as Jesus gives sight to the blind man.

The story opens with Jesus' disciples asking a very rabbinic question. Essentially, they want to know the source of the man's disability. Was it because of his sin or his parents'? The disciples lived their lives by a simple equation: sin = sickness. The only operative question for them in the case of the man born blind was, Whose sin caused the blindness?

Of course it is true that there is a connection between sin and sickness. The problem is that the relationship between the two is not that simple. There is such a thing as innocent suffering. Jesus' response in verse 3 is typical of his outlook on sickness and death. Primarily, they are opportunities for the glory of God to be revealed. (Compare Jesus' outlook on the death of Lazarus in John 11:4.) In verse 4 Jesus implies that his time on earth is limited. While he is still present, he must doggedly accomplish the work the Father has sent him to do. In this particular instance, his work is to faithfully be the light.

The method Jesus uses to heal the man is unique. He spits on the ground and makes mud (see Mk 7:33). Next he places the mud on the man's eyes and sends him to wash at the pool of Siloam, yet another miracle that will happen in absentia.

Many explanations for the use of the spit and mud have been offered. Some say Jesus used spit to heighten the man's expectations since spittle was often used in healing in the first century. There is a fascinating story in Suetonius of Vespasian being asked to spit in the eyes of a blind man.

The story concludes with the healing of the man.[1] Others have suggested that Jesus is reenacting the creation, for God made man from the dust.

A far simpler explanation is obvious when you listen closely to the text. The Pharisees had forbidden spitting on the Sabbath. Specifically they cautioned that the spit might run downhill and make mud, and making mud is work. If you listen closely as the story unfolds and the Pharisees investigate the healing, they are concerned specifically about the mud and the question of who made the mud. As with other healings, they will not be able to recognize a miracle because of their preoccupation with the violation of one of their oral traditions.

The man is obedient to Jesus. He straightforwardly goes, washes and comes home seeing. The response of his neighbors interests John. Some recognize him as the beggar they knew before. Others only claim that he looks like a man. In the midst of the confusion the man is insisting that he is himself!

Compared to the negative portrayal of the man who had been lame for thirty-eight years in John 5, the blind man is endearing. In verse 11 the blind man does something for the first time that he will be called on to do again and again as the story unfolds: explain what had happed to him. Notice in verse 11, unlike the lame man, he has learned Jesus' name. The story is disarmingly simple. Jesus made mud. Put it on his eyes. The blind man washed. He could see. When asked where Jesus is, he replies that he doesn't know. Key to the story is the fact that when he left Jesus, he was still blind. He has never actually seen Jesus.

The Pharisees have heard about the healing and opened an investigation. The central problem is that Jesus made mud on the Sabbath. In verse 15 the man tells his simple story a second time.

As with every other crowd we have encountered in John's Gospel, these Pharisees are divided because of Jesus. Some simply deduced that he is not from God because he broke the Sabbath, the heart and soul of their concept of orthodoxy. Others make the obvious objection, how can a sinner perform such an incredible sign? It sounds like the division between the followers of Hillel and Shammai.

In verse 11 the blind man refers to Jesus as a "man." Now the Pharisees turn to him once more for his opinion of Jesus. Note the progression in verse 17 when he posits that Jesus must be a "prophet."

The investigation is going nowhere, so the man's parents are called in for questioning. They, however, want nothing to do with the whole business. They direct the Pharisees to go back to their son and ask him. In verse 22 John gives a whispered explanation of their motivation. They are aware that a formal ban has been placed on Jesus. Any association with him will result in being put out of the synagogue (compare 12:42).

The ban is far worse than it sounds. It resulted in a person being kicked out not only from a building but from Jewish life altogether. This aspect of the story would have been especially meaningful to John's first readers, who were facing a similar threat of being banned from the synagogues in Ephesus.

In verse 24 the Pharisees solemnly charge the man with an oath. "Give glory to God" is much like our "Tell the truth, the whole truth, and nothing but the truth" (see Josh 7:19). They have concluded that Jesus is a sinner. They are no longer seeking the truth. They are pressuring the man to conform. One of the most endearing aspects of his character is his refusal to do so.

For the third time he tells his simple story. It gets simpler each time he tells it. Now it is simply "I was blind, but now I can see." He possesses a clarity and simplicity that is disturbing to the Pharisees. In verse 26 they ask to hear the story for a fourth time. Specifically they ask "how." That is, they want to hear about how Jesus made the mud.

To his charming simplicity John now adds a touch of humor. The man protests that he has already told them the story. Do they want to hear it again because they somehow desire to become Jesus' disciples too? This is humorous. More to the point, John knows it is humorous when he writes it. His audiences have laughed at this part of the story for years!

The response is completely predictable. The Pharisees are outraged, thinking they have exposed the hoax. The man is actually one of Jesus' disciples. They, on the other hand, are Moses' disciples. They hiss, "We don't even know where he comes from." This is an interesting statement because in John 7:52 they knew Jesus was from Galilee.

The formerly blind man responds to their pressure by advancing another step in his understanding of who Jesus is. He finds it remarkable that the Pharisees know nothing about Jesus, when he was able to heal the man's blindness. Speaking very much like a Pharisee, he reasons that God does not listen to sinners. His next step: Jesus is "from God" or he could do nothing.

In verse 34 the Pharisees give their answer to the question the disciples first asked in verse 2: the man was steeped in sin at birth. They then pronounce the ban and throw him out. From this moment on his parents and friends will have nothing to do with him. He cannot purchase food from any loyal Jew. He is persona non grata.

In verse 35 we see the miracle behind the miracle. Certainly it was amazing to open the eyes of someone born blind. But how much more miraculous is it that Jesus, the Son of God, looks for and finds the man who'd been thrown out of his home and life. Finding him, Jesus asks if he believes in the Son of Man. Remember, he has never actually seen Jesus. In his charming simplicity he responds, "If you tell me, I will believe." It is a cinematic moment. Jesus responds literally, "You are seeing him."

The nameless man makes his final step in realizing who Jesus is when he responds "Lord" in verse 38. Then he worships Jesus.

Jesus concludes that he came into the world for judgment. Note that he did not say he had come to judge the world; Jesus does not condemn as a judge but rather as the light, which by its very presence reveals. The Pharisees, overhearing, retort, "Are we blind too?" When a blind man insists he can see, he places himself outside of the possibility of ever being healed.

JOHN 10

THE GOOD SHEPHERD

10:1–21

A SAFE PLACE BEFORE THE STORM

10:22–42

THE GOOD SHEPHERD

[1]*"I assure you: Anyone who doesn't enter the sheep pen by the door but climbs in some other way, is a thief and a robber.* [2]*The one who enters by the door is the shepherd of the sheep.* [3]*The doorkeeper opens it for him, and the sheep hear his voice. He calls his own sheep by name and leads them out.* [4]*When he has brought all his own outside, he goes ahead of them. The sheep follow him because they recognize his voice.* [5]*They will never follow a stranger; instead they will run away from him, because they don't recognize the voice of strangers."*

[6]*Jesus gave them this illustration, but they did not understand what He was telling them.*

[7]*So Jesus said again, "I assure you: I am the door of the sheep.* [8]*All who came before Me are thieves and robbers, but the sheep didn't listen to them.* [9]*I am the door. If anyone enters by Me, he will be saved and will come in and go out and find pasture.* [10]*A thief comes only to steal and to kill and to destroy. I have come so that they may have life and have it in abundance.*

[11]*"I am the good shepherd. The good shepherd lays down his life for the sheep.* [12]*The hired man, since he is not the shepherd and doesn't own the sheep, leaves them and runs away when he sees a wolf coming. The wolf then snatches and scatters them.* [13]*This happens because he is a hired man and doesn't care about the sheep.*

[14]*"I am the good shepherd. I know My own sheep, and they know Me,* [15]*as the Father knows Me, and I know the Father. I lay down My life for the sheep.* [16]*But I have other sheep that are not of this fold; I must bring them also, and they will listen to My voice. Then there will be one flock, one shepherd.* [17]*This is why the Father loves Me, because I am laying down My life so I may take it up again.* [18]*No one takes it from Me, but I lay it down on My own. I have the right to lay it down, and I have the right to take it up again. I have received this command from My Father."*

[19]*Again a division took place among the Jews because of these words.* [20]*Many of them were saying, "He has a demon and He's crazy! Why do you listen to Him?"* [21]*Others were saying, "These aren't the words of someone demon-possessed. Can a demon open the eyes of the blind?"*

*J*ohn 10:1-21 is a continuation of Jesus' discussion with the Jews after
the controversy surrounding the healing of the man born blind. It will
end in the crowd being divided once again because of Jesus. With chapters 10–11 we rush to the close of Jesus' ministry and on to Passion Week.

Jesus begins with his solemn and enigmatic "amen, amen." Verses 1-6
will establish the images that will be used in his extended illustration.
This is the closest thing to a parable you'll see in the Gospel of John. To
those who accuse Jesus of being purposely obscure, notice that in the
discussion that follows he will use two different metaphors to describe
the nature of his ministry and will repeat each one twice. These are
hardly the words of a person who is trying to be obscure.

Jesus will present himself by means of the image of a shepherd. The
"door for the sheep" is a variation of the same image. He will contrast
himself with two other images representing the Pharisees, who he condemned in John 9:41 as being hopelessly blind. In contrast to the good
shepherd, there are thieves (vv. 1, 10) and hired hands (v. 12). The watch-
man (doorkeeper) of verse 3 is probably John the Baptist, although
"watchmen" is a code word in the Old Testament for the prophets (Hab
2; Ezek 33; see also 1 Pet 2:25; Heb 13:20).

The shepherd calls the sheep to follow him after leading them out.
The only redeeming characteristic of the sheep in this extended allusion
is the fact that they are able to recognize the shepherd's voice and listen
to him. Their principal safety comes in recognizing the stranger's voice
and refusing to follow him. The small clutch of Jewish followers who
have only recently come to believe in Jesus would do well to see that he
is helping them understand how important it is that they learn to stop
listening to and even flee from the thieves, robbers and hired hands,
who represent the Pharisees. But this is John's Gospel, and Jesus has just
spoken a spiritual image, so we can be certain they will not understand.
Which is precisely what happens in verse 6.

Having established the basic image, Jesus will now improvise and
expand. In verses 7-11 he will call himself the gate or door of the sheep.
When we do our homework we learn that this is just another metaphor
for shepherd. All over Palestine the fields are dotted with large circular

stone sheep enclosures. At night the shepherd lies down in the gap, becoming a living door to keep the sheep in and the predators out. The others before him were thieves and robbers, says Jesus. The sheep refused to listen to them, an optimistic projection on the small clutch of newborn followers. Those who enter through him will find salvation, safety and sustenance. The robbers kill. Jesus gives life.

In verses 11-18 Jesus modifies and simplifies the image. He is the good shepherd. Even as he lies down to be the door, so he lays down his life for the sheep. He has begun to plant the seeds of the notion of the upcoming cross. He will progressively reveal in ever-increasing detail exactly what is waiting for him in Jerusalem in a matter of months. In none of the Gospels will his followers understand.

In verses 12-13 the hired hand appears. This is the man who cares nothing for the sheep but is only there to make a day's wage. He will never lay down his life. He can only run when the wolf comes. And the wolf is coming.

In verse 14 Jesus repeats once more that he is the good shepherd. He has mentioned that the sheep know him (v. 4). Now he repeats the concept. He adds that he knows the sheep and ties their relationship of mutual knowing to his relationship with the Father.

Verse 16 looks ahead to the Gentile mission, not a major interest in John's Gospel. Other sheep outside this flock are destined to be folded into this flock. They will someday be one. The last request of Jesus in the Garden of Gethsemane is that we, his followers, become one (Jn 17:22-23). It represents his deep and earnest desire that we put aside our petty divisions and celebrate our unity in him.

The final piece of the image of Jesus as the good shepherd comes in verses 17-18. It is another prefiguring of the cross. His willingness to lay down his life for the sheep is why the Father loves him. He will lay it down voluntarily. No one can take his life away from him by force. No one killed Jesus. He let go of his life voluntarily.

This is the third time now that we have heard that the crowd was divided because of Jesus (see Jn 7:34; 9:16). The charge of demon possession is brought up once more. Again the reasonable ones among the crowd wonder how a demon-possessed man could have opened the eyes of the blind.

In part, the discussion of the good shepherd and the sheep who recognize his voice is a preparation for the story of the raising of Lazarus in chapter 11. Lazarus will become the listening sheep who will recognize the voice of his good shepherd and go through the door of his tomb to life.

A SAFE PLACE BEFORE THE STORM

22Then the Festival of Dedication took place in Jerusalem, and it was winter. 23Jesus was walking in the temple complex in Solomon's Colonnade. 24Then the Jews surrounded Him and asked, "How long are You going to keep us in suspense? If You are the Messiah, tell us plainly."

25"I did tell you and you don't believe," Jesus answered them. "The works that I do in My Father's name testify about Me. 26But you don't believe because you are not My sheep. 27My sheep hear My voice, I know them, and they follow Me. 28I give them eternal life, and they will never perish—ever! No one will snatch them out of My hand. 29My Father, who has given them to Me, is greater than all. No one is able to snatch them out of the Father's hand. 30The Father and I are one."

31Again the Jews picked up rocks to stone Him.

32Jesus replied, "I have shown you many good works from the Father. Which of these works are you stoning Me for?"

33"We aren't stoning You for a good work," the Jews answered, "but for blasphemy, because You—being a man—make Yourself God."

34Jesus answered them, "Isn't it written in your scripture, I said, you are gods? 35If He called those whom the word of God came to 'gods'—and the Scripture cannot be broken— 36do you say, 'You are blaspheming' to the One the Father set apart and sent into the world, because I said: I am the Son of God? 37If I am not doing My Father's works, don't believe Me. 38But if I am doing them and you don't believe Me, believe the works. This way you will know and understand that the Father is in Me and I in the Father." 39Then they were trying again to seize Him, yet He eluded their grasp.

40So He departed again across the Jordan to the place where John had been baptizing earlier, and He remained there. 41Many came to Him and said, "John never did a sign, but everything John said about this man was true." 42And many believed in Him there.

*B*etween verses 21 and 22 there lies a two-month interval. Tabernacles occurs in October. We now see Jesus in Jerusalem once again. John
tells us it is the Feast of Dedication, which we know as Hanukkah. It
happens in the month of December. John states that it is winter. In the
second part of verse 23 he describes a portion of Herod's temple complex known as Solomon's Colonnade, so named because it was believed
to have been built over the actual ruins of Solomon's temple. Notice
how John is concerned for eyewitness details regarding various areas
around the temple complex (Jn 5:2; 7:14, 28; 8:20, 59; 18:1, 28; 19:13, 17).

We were last in the temple with a group of Jewish people who were
divided because of Jesus (v. 19). They have had two months for their
anticipation to build regarding Jesus' true identity. Now they press Jesus
to tell them openly who he is.

When Jesus responds in verses 25-30, we understand why John has
picked up here at this particular time and place. Jesus has returned to
the image of his sheep who hear his voice. The signs have all clearly
pointed to who he is from the changing of water into wine to the healing of the man born blind. It has been made abundantly clear that Jesus
is who he said he was from the beginning. The only feasible explanation
lies in the image of the sheep who hear and recognize his voice, or not.
The Father has given the sheep to him. He and the Father are one. His
miracles have clearly proven his oneness with the Father. Anyone who
fails to see and understand who Jesus is, is represented by the sheep who
do not recognize the voice of the good shepherd. That is the only reasonable explanation.

For the second time the Jews make motions to stone Jesus for his
claim of oneness with the Father (see Jn 8:59). It is clear they understand his reference to the Father as being to God. This is blasphemy,
they claim (v. 33). But Jesus' miracles have all clearly proven his oneness
with the Father. For which one of his miracles, Jesus asks, are they going
to stone him?

Only one other time did Jesus use obscurity to dissuade the crowd,
where he posed a dilemma about whose son the Messiah is (Mt 22:41-
46). Here in John 10:34 he refers to the shortest psalm of Asaph (Ps 82).

It is significant that around the time of the writing of John's Gospel the
Jews were making the final determination to accept the Wisdom writings into the biblical canon, and Jesus is quoted in John as referring to
the shortest of the psalms as the "law" (so NIV; Greek *nomos*). This dem-
onstrates Jesus' regard for the Wisdom books as Scripture.

The angry crowd has accused him of claiming to be one with the
Father, of claiming to be God. But, says Jesus, Asaph says we are all gods.
If the ones who were sent the Word were considered gods, then how
much more the one who is the unique Word of God?

The crowd began by pressuring Jesus to plainly tell who he was. In
verse 36 Jesus makes it clear, he is God's Son. His miracles have consistently proved it. In verse 38 he modifies and reinforces the claim. The
Father is in him and he is in the Father. Clearly Jesus is claiming son-
ship and oneness with God the Father.

The disturbing clarity of his claim is seen by the response of the
crowd. For the second time they make movements to stone him. Once
more without any of the details we crave, John tells us Jesus escaped
their grasp. The implication again: his time had not yet come. Which
further implies: a time is coming for Jesus.

Verses 40-42 represent the calm before the storm. Jesus retreats for
safety to the other side of the Jordan, an area where he spent six months
during the early part of his ministry. Notice he does not retreat to Galilee.
Apparently it is no longer safe for him in his own homeland (see Jn 7:1).

In this final scene before the departure for Jerusalem and the cross,
Jesus is surrounded by a small group of followers. They represent the
sheep he has recently talked about. They have recognized his voice. Their
quality as believers is seen in that they believed John the Baptist, though
he never performed a miraculous sign. This is a significant detail. They
are willing to believe without signs. There are believers in the truest Johannine sense of the word.

JOHN 11

SLEEPING LAZARUS

¹Now a man was sick, Lazarus, from Bethany, the village of Mary and her sister Martha. ²Mary was the one who anointed the Lord with fragrant oil and wiped His feet with her hair, and it was her brother Lazarus who was sick. ³So the sisters sent a message to Him: "Lord, the one You love is sick."

⁴When Jesus heard it, He said, "This sickness will not end in death but is for the glory of God, so that the Son of God may be glorified through it." ⁵Now Jesus loved Martha, her sister, and Lazarus. ⁶So when He heard that he was sick, He stayed two more days in the place where He was. ⁷Then after that, He said to the disciples, "Let's go to Judea again."

⁸"Rabbi," the disciples told Him, "just now the Jews tried to stone You, and You're going there again?"

⁹"Aren't there 12 hours in a day?" Jesus answered. "If anyone walks during the day, he doesn't stumble, because he sees the light of this world. ¹⁰If anyone walks during the night, he does stumble, because the light is not in him." ¹¹He said this, and then He told them, "Our friend Lazarus has fallen asleep, but I'm on My way to wake him up."

¹²Then the disciples said to Him, "Lord, if he has fallen asleep, he will get well."

¹³Jesus, however, was speaking about his death, but they thought He was speaking about natural sleep. ¹⁴So Jesus then told them plainly, "Lazarus has died. ¹⁵I'm glad for you that I wasn't there so that you may believe. But let's go to him."

¹⁶Then Thomas (called "Twin") said to his fellow disciples, "Let's go so that we may die with Him."

The raising of Lazarus is the climactic miracle in the ministry of Jesus in John. It brings together themes that reach all the way back to the prologue (see Jn 1:4; 3:15-16; 5:24, 28; 6:35, 47, 51; 10:10, 28). It will be the miracle that will eventually lead to the cross (v. 53).

As John introduces Lazarus in verses 1-2, he assumes that we already know Mary and Martha. In verse 2 he refers to an event that has not yet occurred, and takes it for granted that we know who Mary is. Perhaps the remarkable story of Jesus memorializing her gift (see Mk 14:6-9) was so well known in the Christian community that John can refer to it before he has presented the story in his own Gospel (Jn 12:3-7).

In the close of chapter 10 we left Jesus with a small band of true be-lievers on the other side of the Jordan. The exact spot is disputed among scholars. Some point to a "Bethany beyond the Jordan" that is only twenty miles away, just across from the city of Jericho. Others point to a location over one hundred miles away, farther north, yet still on the other side of the Jordan. The nearer location makes more sense to me.

Word is sent to Jesus that the "one he loves" is sick. Besides John himself, Lazarus is the only other person to be described this way in John's Gospel. So John is not the only "beloved" disciple. Some have even ventured to say from this reference that Lazarus may have been the author of the Gospel.

When Jesus receives the bad news, he reveals the same point of view he had in John 9:3 when confronted with the man born blind. No, he says, this is for God's glory. Sickness, disease and even death have lost their power, have lost their sting in light of Jesus coming into the world. In him death has simply become a sleep from which he will someday awaken us (Jn 6:39, 40, 44, 54).

Verse 5 serves to explain Jesus' unorthodox response to the bad news. John wants us to know that Jesus truly loved Lazarus and his sisters because what he does in the next verse seems to deny that love. He re-mains there on the other side of the Jordan for two more days! Some-times in our desperation we call out for Jesus to act immediately. Often he delays. The story of Lazarus shows there is always a reason.

Sometime after the two days, Jesus proposes that they go back across the river into Judea. The disciples remind him that people tried to stone him the last time he was there. The truth is, Judea and Jerusalem have been dangerous for Jesus since John 7:1.

Jesus reminds them that he lives his life in a different context. Like the person who walks in daylight and does not stumble, so Jesus must obediently act while his light remains. It is an idea he first spoke in John 9:4-5. It contains a subtle reminder that a time is rapidly approaching when his light will be snuffed out for a brief time.

Without receiving word that Lazarus has died, Jesus tells the disci-ples that he has "fallen asleep." Jesus always refers to death as sleep, and he is always misunderstood (see Mk 5:39). By the time of the book of

Acts, apparently the Christian community had adopted Jesus' unique point of view (Acts 7:60). Lazarus has merely fallen asleep, and now Jesus will go back, at the risk of his own life, to wake him up.

As usual, the disciples misunderstand. Sleep is an indication that the fever has broken and Lazarus will get better. John whispers to us an explanation of their misunderstanding (v. 13). Jesus' response sounds harsh, as harsh as waiting two days when someone you love so badly needs you. He is dead. Jesus is glad he was not there to help. Jesus is glad not for his friend's death but for the opportunity it presents for his disciples to believe. This is the glory he spoke about in verse 4. Their belief is literally more important than life and death.

Though he is mentioned in the other lists of the disciples (Mt 10:3; Mk 3:18; Lk 6:15), Thomas only speaks in John's Gospel. Here, he dolefully remarks that they should go with Jesus so they can die along with him. He will question Jesus in John 14:5 about the way. In John 20 he will display the doubt for which later generations have named him. He is never referred to as "doubting Thomas" in the New Testament.

THE SILENT TEAR

17When Jesus arrived, He found that Lazarus had already been in the tomb four days. 18Bethany was near Jerusalem (about two miles away). 19Many of the Jews had come to Martha and Mary to comfort them about their brother. 20As soon as Martha heard that Jesus was coming, she went to meet Him. But Mary remained seated in the house.

21Then Martha said to Jesus, "Lord, if You had been here, my brother wouldn't have died. 22Yet even now I know that whatever You ask from God, God will give You."

23"Your brother will rise again," Jesus told her.

24Martha said, "I know that he will rise again in the resurrection at the last day."

25Jesus said to her, "I am the resurrection and the life. The one who believes in Me, even if he dies, will live. 26Everyone who lives and believes in Me will never die—ever. Do you believe this?"

27"Yes, Lord," she told Him, "I believe You are the Messiah, the Son of God, who comes into the world."

28Having said this, she went back and called her sister Mary, saying in private, "The Teacher is here and is calling for you."

29As soon as she heard this, she got up quickly and went to Him. 30Jesus had not yet come into the village but was still in the place where Martha had met Him. 31The Jews who were with her in the house consoling her saw that Mary got up quickly and went out. So they followed her, supposing that she was going to the tomb to cry there.

32When Mary came to where Jesus was and saw Him, she fell at His feet and told Him, "Lord, if You had been here, my brother would not have died!"

33When Jesus saw her crying, and the Jews who had come with her crying, He was angry in His spirit and deeply moved. 34"Where have you put him?" He asked.

"Lord," they told Him, "come and see."

35Jesus wept.

36So the Jews said, "See how He loved him!" 37But some of them said, "Couldn't He who opened the blind man's eyes also have kept this man from dying?"

*A*fter Jesus makes his way up the exceedingly steep ridge to Bethany, he receives word that Lazarus has been dead and buried for four days. In the first century the body was placed in the tomb as quickly as possible for obvious reasons. Bethany is just over the Mount of Olives from Jerusalem and John tells us many of their friends had come from the big city to the little village to console the two sisters.

One of the features of Scripture that points to its accuracy is how consistently characters are portrayed over the course of different books. Martha is always herself, as is Mary. Martha hears Jesus has come and, true to character, runs to meet him (see Lk 10:38-42). Her first words to Jesus have the same indignant tone her voice had toward Mary in Luke 10. This is not the first time someone assumed that Jesus only had the gift to heal but lacked the power to raise someone from the dead (see Lk 7:49). It is crystal clear to Martha in her black-and-white world. If Jesus had been there, he could have saved her brother. Then, all of a sudden, it seems that she says more than she knows, certainly more than she believes. Even now God will

give Jesus whatever he asks. Jesus' response is simple and straightforward. Her brother will rise.

The rabbis later taught that those who did not believe in the resurrection would not share in the life to come.[1] Perhaps Martha has already
heard this teaching. She confirms to Jesus her belief in the resurrection
at the last day. But resurrection is no longer a matter of a time or a place,
but a person. Jesus is the resurrection. Not a theological abstraction but
a living, breathing human being. It is one of his most disturbing habits,
positing himself as the answer to a question or problem. It means that
he is either a madman or the Son of God. There is no gray area; he has
not left us with one.

Jesus straightforwardly asks Martha if she believes this unbelievable
message. Again, speaking more than she knows, she confesses him to be
the Christ and the Son of God. Martha is not the one-dimensional
cartoon character she has so often been reduced to in stories and sermons. She is a forceful, determined woman of faith. Today we would
characterize her as being left-brained, practical, the kind of person who
gets things done.

She sends word back home to Mary that Jesus has come and is asking
for her. Interestingly, Martha refers to Jesus as the "Teacher" (*didaskalos*).
Mary jumps up and runs to the edge of town where Jesus, her dear
friend, awaits. Her friends assume she has gone to the tomb to mourn.
The first week after death was set aside for "deep grief" for the family.

When Mary reaches Jesus she does what she consistently does in all
of the Gospels, she falls at his feet (Mt 28:9; Lk 10:39; Jn 11:2; 12:3). Notice that Mary speaks the identical words Martha had spoken before (v.
21), but when she speaks them, they have a totally different effect on
Jesus. Before, Martha seemed almost to be scolding. Mary, on her knees,
almost certainly says the words through her tears. When Jesus sees her
weeping, as well as her friends that have followed her, he shudders (v. 33).
The Greek word *embrinaomai* originally described a horse snorting.
Jesus is shaken by their grief, by another experience of the death-
impregnated world. Perhaps he is even realizing that in a matter of days
he will be the one who is dead and in the tomb.

As Jesus joins Mary and the others on the way to the tomb, John says simply, Jesus wept. The word used here, *edakrysen*, appears only here in the New Testament. It comes from the Greek word for "tear" and depicts silently crying; the image is of a solitary tear falling down the cheek. The word used to describe the weeping of Mary and her friends, *klaio*, describes an outburst of crying (v. 33).

I am tempted to see their explanation of Jesus' tears in verse 36 as another instance of the motif of misunderstanding. The crowd simply believes that Jesus weeps because of his great love. Perhaps that is true. But I tend to hear their statement as a misunderstanding of the true depth of his grief. He knows he is going to raise Lazarus. Perhaps his tears go deeper, to the heart of the fall. Perhaps they give evidence to his deep emotional connection with Mary and her grief (Rom 12:15).

Before they reach the tomb, a statement from someone in the crowd speaks volumes. It reveals their level of expectation that was consistent throughout Jesus' ministry. It was first revealed in Martha's statement. It was a fairly well-accepted fact that he could heal, but no one believed he had the power to raise someone from the dead. After the resurrection there will be a completely new level of expectation. In the book of Acts after Tabitha passes away, they call for Peter (Acts 9:36-43).

"LET HIM GO"

[38] *Then Jesus, angry in Himself again, came to the tomb. It was a cave, and a stone was lying against it.* [39] *"Remove the stone," Jesus said.*

Martha, the dead man's sister, told Him, "Lord, he's already decaying. It's been four days."

[40] *Jesus said to her, "Didn't I tell you that if you believed you would see the glory of God?"*

[41] *So they removed the stone. Then Jesus raised His eyes and said, "Father, I thank You that You heard Me.* [42] *I know that You always hear Me, but because of the crowd standing here I said this, so they may believe You sent Me."* [43] *After He said this, He shouted with a loud voice, "Lazarus, come out!"* [44] *The dead man came out, bound hand and foot with linen strips and with his face wrapped in a cloth. Jesus said to them, "Loose him and let him go."*

*A*s they reach the tomb, John repeats the word he used earlier to describe Jesus' emotion in verse 33. He shudders once again. Lazarus's body has been wrapped up and placed in a cave with a stone to cover the door. This is stage one of the two-staged Jewish burial. In a year's time Mary and Martha would have returned to the tomb to gather the bones, wash them and place them in an ossuary or bone box. Lazarus is not going to need step two for now.

When Jesus orders the tomb open, Martha, always the practical person, reminds him that by day four the smell is going to be unbearable. Jesus persists and the stone is removed. At this point he goes to prayer. All miracles are only answered prayers. He looks up to the Father. He is confident that he is always heard when he prays. In fact, it seems he is only crying out loud so the bystanders will hear what he is saying and believe.

In John 10:27 Jesus had pointed out that his sheep will hear his voice and that they will pass through the gate to life. This moment is a living parable of that truth. He shouts in a loud voice to his beloved friend and calls him out of the tomb. And the "dead man" obliges. He has no choice. Jesus has absolute authority, and Lazarus is one of his obedient sheep.

Lazarus is wrapped up in a shroud with a separate "sweat cloth" (*soudarion*) around his face. Jesus, perhaps in disgust at the grave clothes and their constriction, or maybe with a triumphant tone, commands that the people "Let him go."

THE PLOT

⁴⁵Therefore, many of the Jews who came to Mary and saw what He did believed in Him. ⁴⁶But some of them went to the Pharisees and told them what Jesus had done.

⁴⁷So the chief priests and the Pharisees convened the Sanhedrin and said, "What are we going to do since this man does many signs? ⁴⁸If we let Him continue in this way, everyone will believe in Him! Then the Romans will come and remove both our place and our nation."

⁴⁹One of them, Caiaphas, who was high priest that year, said to them, "You know nothing at all! ⁵⁰You're not considering that it is to your advantage that one man should die for the people rather than the whole nation perish."

⁵¹He did not say this on his own, but being high priest that year he prophesied that Jesus was going to die for the nation, ⁵²and not for the nation only, but also to unite the scattered children of God. ⁵³So from that day on they plotted to kill Him. ⁵⁴Therefore Jesus no longer walked openly among the Jews but departed from there to the countryside near the wilderness, to a town called Ephraim. And He stayed there with the disciples.

⁵⁵The Jewish Passover was near, and many went up to Jerusalem from the country to purify themselves before the Passover. ⁵⁶They were looking for Jesus and asking one another as they stood in the temple complex: "What do you think? He won't come to the festival, will He?" ⁵⁷The chief priests and the Pharisees had given orders that if anyone knew where He was, he should report it so they could arrest Him.

*T*he miracle causes an immediate response. Many of the eyewitnesses believe in Jesus. The Sanhedrin calls an emergency meeting.

John's inside information as to what was said behind the closed doors of the Sanhedrin almost certainly came from either Nicodemus or Joseph of Arimathea. Verse 48 is significant. It speaks of the true motivation of this powerful body. They are afraid of the Romans. If Jesus causes an uproar, the Romans will come and take away their "place." The Pharisees referred to the temple as *ha makom*, literally "the Place." Their fears will be realized in A.D. 70 when the Romans will do just that, burn the temple to the ground and exile every last Jew from Jerusalem.

In verse 49 we hear Caiaphas's name and voice for the first time. John refers to him more than all of the other Gospels combined. He was high priest from A.D. 18–36, a remarkably long tenure at a time when the Romans were investing and deposing high priests every few years. Josephus comments on the arrogance of the high priests.² Caiaphas's tone confirms this. He tells the august body of the wisest men in Israel that they know nothing: it is better for one man to die than for the whole nation to perish.

John whispers the explanation to us in verses 51-52. Caiaphas was trying to fulfill his own prophecy. So out of fear of the Romans and Jesus the Sanhedrin decides to take Jesus' life, a violation of the sixth commandment (Ex 20:13). In John 12:10 they will include Lazarus in the plot, for he is a dangerous piece of living evidence. At this point the Sanhedrin should have been a divided body. There are at least a few Pharisees in the group who adamantly believe in the resurrection, which the Sadducees, who make up most of the Sanhedrin, deny. By raising Lazarus Jesus has given the Pharisees the best proof of resurrection they can hope to have. Yet it seems that their hatred and fear of Jesus is greater than their desire to demonstrate the truth of what they believe about the resurrection.

In verse 54 we see Jesus hiding for the third time. He retreats twenty miles to the north of Jerusalem to a village called Ephraim. There he will stay with his disciples. Verses 55-57 provide the final prelude for the Passion Week. Once more John places us in the middle of the whispering crowd who is looking for Jesus and wondering when he will appear (see Jn 7:11). Again we are reminded of the formal ban that has been pronounced against Jesus (see Jn 9:22). When Jesus enters Jerusalem in just one week's time, it will be as a man who has already been condemned.

JOHN 12

OVER-THE-TOP LOVE

12:1–11

A ROYAL ENTRY

12:12–19

THE FINAL SIGN

12:20–36

THE CONTEXT

12:37–50

OVER-THE-TOP LOVE

¹Six days before the Passover, Jesus came to Bethany where Lazarus was, the one Jesus had raised from the dead. ²So they gave a dinner for Him there; Martha was serving them, and Lazarus was one of those reclining at the table with Him. ³Then Mary took a pound of fragrant oil—pure and expensive nard—anointed Jesus' feet, and wiped His feet with her hair. So the house was filled with the fragrance of the oil.

⁴Then one of His disciples, Judas Iscariot (who was about to betray Him), said, ⁵"Why wasn't this fragrant oil sold for 300 denarii, and given to the poor?" ⁶He didn't say this because he cared about the poor but because he was a thief. He was in charge of the money-bag and would steal part of what was put in it.

⁷Jesus answered, "Leave her alone; she has kept it for the day of My burial. ⁸For you always have the poor with you, but you do not always have Me."

⁹Then a large crowd of the Jews learned He was there. They came not only because of Jesus, but also to see Lazarus the one He had raised from the dead. ¹⁰Therefore the chief priests decided to kill Lazarus also ¹¹because he was the reason many of the Jews were deserting them and believing in Jesus.

Chapter 12 resumes roughly a month after the raising of Lazarus. Six days before Passover makes the date Friday, March 27, 33. In just one day Jesus will enter Jerusalem, and the Passion Week will begin, the final week of his earthly ministry.

He has returned to Bethany for a party someone has given in his honor. Both Mark and Matthew, who also tell the story of the anointing, give the detail that the banquet took place in the home of Simon the Leper (Mt 26:6; Mk 14:3). Who was Simon? All we can do is guess at this point, since there are no other details provided. Perhaps Simon had been healed by Jesus, otherwise they would hardly be having a party at his home. There was a leper colony just outside the village of Bethany. The party might have been a celebration of his healing. Since Lazarus and his sisters are there and Martha is serving (v. 2), there is a chance that they may have been related. Whatever the unknown details might be, it gladdens the heart that someone thought to give a party to honor Jesus.

Lazarus is reclining, Hellenistic style, with the other guests, while Martha, true to character, is serving. At some point during the meal Mary appears with an alabaster jar (Mt 26:7; Mk 14:3). John is not interested in what the jar is made of. It contains nard, a rosy-colored, sweet-smelling perfume that comes from a plant which grows in the foothills of the Himalayas. This hints at its enormous value. Only John tells us that she poured out about twelve ounces of the precious ointment on Jesus' feet, wiping his feet with her hair. (The Greek word *litra* denotes a Roman pound, which is 324 grams or 12 ounces.)

We already know Mary to be an extraordinary woman (Lk 10:38-42). We always find her at Jesus' feet learning, serving or weeping. The perfume was most likely an heirloom handed down from her mother to Mary. It is worth 300 denarii. The denarius was the standard day's wage. So the value of the ointment is worth roughly a year's wages, according to Judas. For his betrayal of Jesus, Judas receives 30 pieces of silver, worth roughly $3,000. At the moment Mary is pouring on Jesus' feet ointment worth approximately $30,000. So this is the exchange rate between love and betrayal: 10 to 1.

To have poured perfume on Jesus' head would have been extravagant enough, but Mary pours it on his feet and wipes his feet with her own hair. It was an over-the-top demonstration of absolute devotion to Jesus. Both Matthew and Mark record Jesus memorializing her actions, claiming that it will become a part of the gospel message whenever it is told throughout the world. John omits the memorial but adds a sense memory in the second sentence of verse 3. He remembers that the fragrance of the perfume filled the house. That detail has no other purpose except to allow us to be present in the story through our imaginations. Sense memories involving smell are the most powerful connections we can have to our past.

Judas's objection to what seemed a great waste provides a small window into his character. John takes us aside and explains his motivation. He did not object because he cared for the poor. He simply wanted more money in the bag he had been entrusted with, more money from which to steal. This is consistent with his character as portrayed in Matthew 26:15. Here Judas goes to the priests and asks, "What are you willing to give me if I hand Him over to you?" Again, the accuracy of the Scriptures is revealed in the consistent portrayal of characters through different books.

Jesus seems to always stand up for Mary (see Lk 10:42). "Leave her alone," he tells Judas. He reminds them, according to Deuteronomy 15:11, that the poor will always be there, but he will not. It is the first of two warnings in the chapter that he will not be with them much longer (see also v. 35).

John concludes the story with an outward look. A large crowd of curiosity seekers has come to see this Jesus they had heard so much about. They have also come to gawk at Lazarus, the "dead man." Because Lazarus's name has become associated with Jesus, the priests make plans to kill him as well. Jesus is a dangerous person to know in Jerusalem.

A ROYAL ENTRY

12 The next day, when the large crowd that had come to the festival heard that Jesus was coming to Jerusalem, 13they took palm branches and went out to meet Him. They kept shouting: "Hosanna! He who comes in the name of the Lord is the blessed One—the King of Israel!"

14Jesus found a young donkey and sat on it, just as it is written: 15Fear no more, Daughter Zion. Look, your King is coming, sitting on a donkey's colt.

16His disciples did not understand these things at first. However, when Jesus was glorified, then they remembered that these things had been written about Him and that they had done these things to Him. 17Meanwhile, the crowd, which had been with Him when He called Lazarus out of the tomb and raised him from the dead, continued to testify. 18This is also why the crowd met Him, because they heard He had done this sign.

19Then the Pharisees said to one another, "You see? You've accomplished nothing. Look—the world has gone after Him!"

*T*he next day Jesus enters the city along with the Passover crowd. The population of Jerusalem, estimated to have been approximately 250,000 in Jesus' day, swelled to almost 1,000,000 during Passover. The band of followers surrounding Jesus would have been a momentary blip on the radar screen for the Roman soldiers keeping an eye on the enormous stream of pilgrims entering the city.

Jesus is surrounded by people waving palm branches, carried up the ridge from Jericho, the "City of the Palms." The palm branch was a national symbol, appearing on Jewish national coins. The people are shouting out the exclamation "Hosanna!" which translates "Oh, save." They are also calling out the standard Passover greeting, "Blessed is he who comes in the name of the Lord," only the greeting is focused on Jesus in a particular way with the addition of the phrase, "Blessed is the king of Israel." Without question, Jesus is entering the city as a royal figure.

In verse 14 the image becomes even more certain as Jesus finds a young donkey to sit on. This is a fulfillment of Zechariah 9:9, a promise that the King who was to come would be riding a donkey's colt.

It is a chaotic moment filled with emotion and mixed motives. John takes us aside in verse 16 and explains that the disciples did not understand at the moment what all of the adulation and the prophetic signs meant. It was not until Jesus was risen and glorified that they realized its meaning and that they had actually done these things to Jesus.

As he had done in verse 9, again, John steps back and analyzes the crowd (v. 17). They are still talking about Lazarus and the miracle of his resurrection from the dead. The word of it is still spreading among the people, and they are responding by coming out to meet Jesus. Clearly, to the Pharisees it is all getting out of hand. In typical rabbinic hyperbole they complain that the "whole world" has gone after Jesus (see *b. Yoma* 71b; Acts 17:6).

THE FINAL SIGN

20Now some Greeks were among those who went up to worship at the festival. 21So they came to Philip, who was from Bethsaida in Galilee, and requested of him, "Sir, we want to see Jesus."

22Philip went and told Andrew; then Andrew and Philip went and told Jesus. 23Jesus replied to them, "The hour has come for the Son of Man to be glorified.

24"I assure you: Unless a grain of wheat falls to the ground and dies, it remains by itself. But if it dies, it produces a large crop. 25The one who loves his life will lose it, and the one who hates his life in this world will keep it for eternal life. [26] If anyone serves Me, he must follow Me. Where I am, there My servant also will be. If anyone serves Me, the Father will honor him.

[27] "Now My soul is troubled. What should I say—Father, save Me from this hour? But that is why I came to this hour. [28] Father, glorify Your name!"

Then a voice came from heaven: "I have glorified it, and I will glorify it again!"

[29] The crowd standing there heard it and said it was thunder. Others said that an angel had spoken to Him.

[30] Jesus responded, "This voice came, not for Me, but for you. [31] Now is the judgment of this world. Now the ruler of this world will be cast out. [32] As for Me, if I am lifted up from the earth I will draw all people to Myself." [33] He said this to signify what kind of death He was about to die.

[34] Then the crowd replied to Him, "We have heard from the scripture that the Messiah will remain forever. So how can You say, 'The Son of Man must be lifted up'? Who is this Son of Man?"

[35] Jesus answered, "The light will be with you only a little longer. Walk while you have the light so that darkness doesn't overtake you. The one who walks in darkness doesn't know where he's going. [36] While you have the light, believe in the light so that you may become sons of light." Jesus said this, then went away and hid from them.

*A*t this point the Synoptic Gospels tell the story of the second temple expulsion. John has already provided us with the unique account of the first expulsion in John 2:12-25. Here, John provides one of his significant substitutions. Though he does not tell the story of Jesus driving the traders from the Court of the Gentiles, he does show us the result of Jesus' courageous action—the coming of the Greeks.

Perhaps the Pharisees were right and the whole world was coming to Jesus. Here, in verse 20, a group of Gentile Greeks ask to meet with Jesus. By clearing out the marketplace from the court of the Gentiles, Jesus had reestablished a quiet place for prayer for them. Perhaps they are coming to thank him. They come first to Philip, presumably because he has a Greek name. The detail that they had come to worship at the feast indicates that they are "God fearers," that is, Gentiles who worship the God of Israel but will not become full proselytes (see Acts 17:4).

Throughout the story the comment has been made that Jesus' time had not yet come. In verse 23, from Jesus' own lips the pronouncement is made: the hour *has* come. There is no more detail in regard to the coming of the Greeks. They have served their purpose. They were the sign Jesus had been looking for. The Gentile world has come knocking. It was an indication to Jesus that the time for the cross had come.

Verses 23-28 sound almost like a soliloquy:

"The kernel must fall into the ground and die."
"The man who hates his life will keep it."
"Whoever serves me must follow me."

Here Jesus makes one of his most encouraging statements to his followers, though most of us read right past it: "If anyone serves Me, the Father will honor him." It could almost be Shakespeare, "Now is my soul troubled." Jesus has begun the struggle with his Father's will that will finally be won in the garden.

All at once another voice interrupts Jesus' sorrow. Some of the people there thought it sounded like thunder. Others apparently could make out the sound of words and attributed the voice to an angel. Jesus responds sadly to the confusion. The voice was not for his sake but theirs. It comes in response to Jesus' words in verse 28, "Father, glorify your name." The voice that sounds like thunder echoes that he has glorified his name and will glorify it again (compare 8:54).

Remembering the hour had come, Jesus reiterates that now is the time for judgment on the world. It is time for the world's sin to be judged and found guilty. The penalty for the guilt will be poured out on Jesus. The result will be that the world will be drawn to him and the prince of the world will be driven out.

Perhaps he still has in mind the final sign of the coming of the Greeks when he says he will draw "all people" to himself when he is "lifted up." "Lifted up" is always a metaphor for crucifixion (see Jn 3:14). This is one of the most commonly misunderstood sayings of Jesus. Here, "lifted up" does not mean to be praised or worshiped. Yet many interpret this passage saying, "Jesus said if we lift him up (i.e., worship him), all men would be drawn to him." Verse 33 makes it clear. He said this to show

how he would die, that he would be crucified, that is, lifted up. It is a part of our calling certainly to worship Jesus. But he never said that by worshiping him all people would be drawn to him.

The crowd misunderstands Jesus' emotional statement. The reference to crucifixion was clear to them, however. Their misunderstanding is that they thought the law said the Messiah would live forever (see Ps 89:36-37). How can Jesus say he is going to be crucified?

In verse 35 Jesus utters his second warning (see also v. 8). It is reminiscent of the warning he gave the disciples in John 11:9. The light will not last forever. While you have the chance, put your trust in the light.

Having just come out of hiding in John 11:54, now Jesus returns to hiding. If he is to fulfill the work of the One who sent him, he must walk softly for now.

THE CONTEXT

37Even though He had performed so many signs in their presence, they did not believe in Him. 38But this was to fulfill the word of Isaiah the prophet, who said:

> *Lord, who has believed our message?*
> *And who has the arm of the Lord*
> *been revealed to?*

39This is why they were unable to believe, because Isaiah also said:

> *40He has blinded their eyes*
> *and hardened their hearts,*
> *so that they would not see with their eyes*
> *or understand with their hearts,*
> *and be converted,*
> *and I would heal them.*

41Isaiah said these things because he saw His glory and spoke about Him. 42Nevertheless, many did believe in Him even among the rulers, but because of the Pharisees they did not confess Him, so they would not be banned from the synagogue. 43For they loved praise from men more than praise from God. 44Then Jesus cried out, "The one who believes in Me believes not in Me, but in Him who sent Me. [45]And the one who sees Me sees Him who sent Me. [46]I have come as a light into the world, so that everyone who believes in Me would not remain in darkness. [47]If anyone hears My words and doesn't keep them, I do not judge him; for I did not come to judge the world but to save the world. [48]The one who rejects Me and doesn't accept My sayings has this as his judge: The word I have spoken will judge him on the last day. [49]For I have not spoken on My own, but the Father Himself who sent Me has given Me a command as to what I should say and what I should speak. [50]I know that His command is eternal life. So the things that I speak, I speak just as the Father has told Me."

*V*erses 37-40 spell out the context of stubborn disbelief that has surrounded Jesus throughout his ministry. They had seen blind eyes opened, thousands fed, the dead raised to life, and yet they still refused to believe in him. Isaiah had asked the rhetorical question, "Who has believed our message?" (Is 53:1). The truth is they refused to believe, even though they kept demanding signs even up to the last moment (see Mt 27:42).

Next, John quotes another passage from Isaiah. This verse is quoted five times in the New Testament (Mt 13:13; Mk 4:12; Lk 8:10; Jn 12:40; Acts 28:26). It is often misunderstood to mean that God has deliberately blinded the eyes and hearts of the people. The key is the context of stubborn disbelief that existed at the time of Isaiah and that is established in Jesus' time by verse 37. Paul explains the process in Romans 1:18-32. After the people continually refuse to believe, in spite of God's reaching out to them again and again, God gives them over to blindness and hardened hearts. Isaiah said this, says John, because he saw Jesus' glory and spoke about him (Is 6:1, 3, 5).

In the midst of the discussion of hardness of heart many of the leaders believed in Jesus (v. 42). Once again we are reminded of the ban that so many feared (Jn 9:22). For now many would remain silent believers. After the cross, at least two of them will boldly claim and bury the body of Jesus: Nicodemus and Joseph.

Listen closely to verses 44-50. Jesus is summing up. It is the last public pronouncement of his ministry. In the following chapters we will have an extended private time of instruction and encouragement between Jesus and the disciples. He is shouting once more (Jn 7:37). He is proclaiming one last time his oneness with the Father, who sent him. It is the final proclamation of who he is. He is the light (v. 46); he is the one who refuses to pass judgment though he has been given the authority to judge (v. 47). He is the one who only spoke the words the Father had given him to speak (v. 49). His final statement is pointed and deliberate: "So whatever I say is just what the Father has told me to say" (v. 50 NIV).

They are the perfect words to bring the ministry to a close.

JOHN 13

THE FULL EXTENT OF HIS LOVE

¹Before the Passover Festival, Jesus knew that His hour had come to depart from this world to the Father. Having loved His own who were in the world, He loved them to the end.

²Now by the time of supper, the Devil had already put it into the heart of Judas, Simon Iscariot's son, to betray Him. ³Jesus knew that the Father had given everything into His hands, that He had come from God, and that He was going back to God. ⁴So He got up from supper, laid aside His robe, took a towel, and tied it around Himself. ⁵Next, He poured water into a basin and began to wash His disciples' feet and to dry them with the towel tied around Him.

⁶He came to Simon Peter, who asked Him, "Lord, are You going to wash my feet?"

⁷Jesus answered him, "What I'm doing you don't understand now, but afterward you will know."

⁸"You will never wash my feet—ever!" Peter said.

Jesus replied, "If I don't wash you, you have no part with Me."

⁹Simon Peter said to Him, "Lord, not only my feet, but also my hands and my head."

¹⁰"One who has bathed," Jesus told him, "doesn't need to wash anything except his feet, but he is completely clean. You are clean, but not all of you." ¹¹For He knew who would betray Him. This is why He said, "You are not all clean."

¹²When Jesus had washed their feet and put on His robe, He reclined again and said to them, "Do you know what I have done for you? ¹³You call Me Teacher and Lord. This is well said, for I am. ¹⁴So if I, your Lord and Teacher, have washed your feet, you also ought to wash one another's feet. ¹⁵For I have given you an example that you also should do just as I have done for you.

¹⁶"I assure you: A slave is not greater than his master, and a messenger is not greater than the one who sent him. ¹⁷If you know these things, you are blessed if you do them."

*A*t this point in the story of Jesus we should be reading the accounts of the Last Supper, but John has omitted it. He always makes a significant substitution, giving us information none of the other Gospels provide. Here he substitutes what happens after the supper, when Jesus washed the feet of the disciples. The context for the foot washing is found in Luke 22:24, where we are told that the disciples have been arguing once more about which one of them is the greatest. This background makes the story of Jesus washing their feet clear. Jesus had interrupted more than one such argument (Mt 18:1; 23:11; Mk 8:34; Lk 9:46; 22:24).

The washing of the disciples' feet is another lived out parable in John's Gospel. Jesus finally gives up on words. He has spoken the truth to them: the greatest must become the servant. Now he will enact the truth for them. All of us must see the truth lived out and not simply spoken if we are ever to fully understand. Significantly, after this moment, they never again argue about who the greatest is!

Jesus and his disciples were celebrating the Passover meal. According to diaspora tradition, Galilean Jews celebrated the meal on Thursday night instead of the prescribed Friday. This explains why there is no reference to a lamb at their meal.[1] It also explains the apparent discrepancy between their celebrating the Passover now and the fact that the Judean Jews are anxious to get Jesus off the cross on Friday evening so they can celebrate their Passover (Jn 19:31). The truth is, there are two separate observances in play, one Galilean, the other Judean.

John, so preoccupied with the meaning of love, introduces the story by saying this was Jesus' way of showing them the "full extent" of his love. That Jesus can demonstrate to his men the full extent of his infinite love for them by doing something as apparently insignificant as washing their feet makes this moment one of his most significant miracles.

The context and the miracle itself are provided in just four verses (vv. 2-6). Judas had already listened to the prompting of the devil. Matthew tells us he had gone to the high priest six days earlier and made arrangements to betray Jesus (Mt 26:14-16).

In verse 3 John gives us three truths that are behind the foot washing. Jesus realizes that the Father had given him absolute power, that he had come from God, and that he would soon be returning to God. If this had ever been true of any other person in all the human race, their response would've been predictable; they would declare themselves sovereign over all the earth! But when Jesus quietly becomes aware of these three truths he responds differently, paradoxically. The *so* which opens verse 4 provides the connection. It might be translated "therefore." Having realized his ultimate power and unique origin with God, he gets up from the table and changes his appearance to that of a slave by taking off his robe and wrapping a towel around his waist. He makes the deliberate preparations of pouring water into a basin. Imagine the stunned silence of the disciples at this point. Then, one by one, methodically and deliberately he goes to each of them and on his knees washes their feet. Judas included. (Judas does not leave the room until verse 30.)

Peter is amazingly silent in John's Gospel. When he was called in John 1:41-42, he did not utter a word. The only time he speaks before this moment is in John 6:68 when, confronted with Jesus' question, "Do you want to leave too?" He responds, "Who will we go to?"

Once more the portrayal of Peter's character is consistent. He is always himself. His question in verse 6 seems filled with surprise. Perhaps he thought Jesus would wash everyone else's feet but his. Jesus calmly responds that even though he doesn't understand, he will later (see also Jn 12:16). Pulling away, Peter, very much himself at this point, says literally, "You will never, into the age, wash my feet." As far as Peter is concerned, what Jesus is doing is completely inappropriate. From a simpler point of view, he is absolutely right.

Jesus, surely tired by this point, still patiently responds that if Peter does not "get" this, he does not "get" Jesus. Peter's willing acceptance of the servanthood and humility of Jesus are the basis for his own discipleship. You might call this a "deal breaker," as far as Jesus is concerned. If you do not know Jesus as your Servant Lord, you do not really know him.

Peter receives the message loud and clear. He is prepared to make one of his Petrine about-faces. Now he wants a bath! Listen closely to his response. It reveals a heart that is fully committed. If the foot washing is necessary, then he wants a full immersion bath. Peter is never half way, never lukewarm. The mature disciple we come to know in the book of Acts lives out this same extreme dedication and devotion.

Jesus, convinced of Peter's sincerity for the moment, calms his impetuosity. He is clean because of the word Jesus has spoken (Jn 15:3). For now, the foot washing is enough. But it will not be enough for Judas.

In verses 12-17 we can see Jesus doing something he never does for the crowd and rarely does even for his disciples. He explains himself. Returning to his place at the three-sided table, he asks if they understand what he has just done. Notice, he does not seem to wait for a response because they are still gobsmacked by what he has just done.

It is very simple: he is their Lord and Teacher. If the most significant and important member of the group has set an example of humility by washing their feet, they should reciprocate and do the same. The foot washing was a lived out example of what it means to be the greatest in the kingdom. Speaking in second person, he sums up: no servant (them) is greater than his master (Jesus), nor is a messenger (Jesus) greater than the one who sent him (the Father). This is the most unanticipated and paradoxical characteristic of Jesus' upside-down kingdom. The Lord of glory will serve and suffer and die for his disciples. What then should their response to such love be? Certainly, not lording it over each other by jockeying for the most important position. Greatness in Jesus' value system is making oneself small, becoming a slave who has given up his or her choices. Jesus closes the initial phase of this discourse by promising them all a blessing if they will do these things.

AND IT WAS NIGHT

¹⁸ *"I'm not speaking about all of you; I know those I have chosen. But the Scripture must be fulfilled: The one who eats My bread has raised his heel against Me.*

¹⁹ *"I am telling you now before it happens, so that when it does happen you will believe that I am He. ²⁰I assure you: Whoever receives anyone I send receives Me, and the one who receives Me receives Him who sent Me."*

²¹ *When Jesus had said this, He was troubled in His spirit and testified, "I assure you: One of you will betray Me!"*

²² *The disciples started looking at one another—uncertain which one He was speaking about. ²³One of His disciples, the one Jesus loved, was reclining close beside Jesus. ²⁴Simon Peter motioned to him to find out who it was He was talking about. ²⁵So he leaned back against Jesus and asked Him, "Lord, who is it?"*

²⁶Jesus replied, "He's the one I give the piece of bread to after I have dipped it." When He had dipped the bread, He gave it to Judas, Simon Iscariot's son. ²⁷After Judas ate the piece of bread, Satan entered him. Therefore Jesus told him, "What you're doing, do quickly."

²⁸None of those reclining at the table knew why He told him this. ²⁹Since Judas kept the money-bag, some thought that Jesus was telling him, "Buy what we need for the festival," or that he should give something to the poor. ³⁰After receiving the piece of bread, he went out immediately. And it was night.

*J*ohn devotes more verses to the betrayal of Judas than any of the other Gospels. Here in verses 18-30, he will go into great detail concerning the discussion between Jesus and the disciples regarding Judas's betrayal.

It is significant that the betrayal is prefigured in Psalm 41:9. Jesus quotes the verse concerning the friend who shares his bread, as Judas literally takes the bread from Jesus' own hand (v. 26). The image of lifting up the heel in Semitic culture speaks of betrayal and disdain. To show someone the bottom of your foot is a mark of contempt.

Jesus has quoted a psalm that alludes to betrayal. He has hinted that not every one of them is clean (v. 11). In verse 19 he refers to something he is telling them now, yet still he hasn't really told them. If he were too obvious, Judas might not make it out of the room alive. In verse 21 Jesus is literally "troubled in his spirit." It is almost as if he cannot hold it in any longer. They need to know that one of them is going to betray him.

Verse 22 was the basis of Leonardo da Vinci's famous *Last Supper* fresco. Not easily rendered speechless, the Twelve do not know what to say in response to Jesus' prediction of betrayal. At this point John identifies himself for all time as the "disciple whom Jesus loved." Reclining at his right side, he can lean against Jesus and whisper, "Lord, who is it?" after Peter motioned from the other side of the room to ask Jesus which one it was. (In John 21:20 this moment will be used to identify the author of the Gospel.)

As a secret sign to John, Jesus says it is the one to whom he will hand the bread after dipping it in the Passover relish. This would indicate that Judas is sitting on Jesus' immediate left. In Judaism this was referred to as the place of the intimate friend. There is a possibility that Jesus and Judas were far closer friends than any of the Gospels can bring themselves to say. The moment Jesus hands the bread to Judas, John says, "Satan entered him."

Jesus tells Judas to do quickly what he was about to do. Since Judas had taken charge of the money and was so adamant earlier about giving to the poor (Jn 12:5), the disciples assume he was going to offer charity, to give some money away, not to make money. Judas takes the bread and goes. The next time they will see him will be in the garden leading a detachment of soldiers.

It is too symbolic a moment for John not to resort to some literary symbolism. Throughout the Gospel, from the very first (Jn 1:4-5) light has been one of his major themes. Now as Judas slithers off into the night, John cannot help but sound the dark literary note "And it was night."

LOVE ONE ANOTHER

³¹*When he had gone out, Jesus said, "Now the Son of Man is glorified, and God is glorified in Him.* ³²*If God is glorified in Him, God will also glorify Him in Himself and will glorify Him at once.*

³³*"Children, I am with you a little while longer. You will look for Me, and just as I told the Jews, 'Where I am going you cannot come,' so now I tell you.*

³⁴*"I give you a new command: Love one another. Just as I have loved you, you must also love one another.* ³⁵*By this all people will know that you are My disciples, if you have love for one another."*

³⁶*"Lord," Simon Peter said to Him, "where are You going?"*

Jesus answered, "Where I am going you cannot follow Me now, but you will follow later."

³⁷*"Lord," Peter asked, "why can't I follow You now? I will lay down my life for You!"*

³⁸*Jesus replied, "Will you lay down your life for Me? I assure you: A rooster will not crow until you have denied Me three times."*

*T*he mood must have radically changed after Judas left, if for no one else but Jesus. With the sky darkening outside and Judas moving off into that darkness, himself a part of that darkness, Jesus' mind turns to glory.

As he understands things, now he is glorified and God is glorified as well. An inescapable series of events began with the simple act of handing Judas the bread and telling him to go. Jesus is committed fully to ride out these dark events.

In what must have been their most intense and intimate moment, Jesus refers to the Eleven by a term he uses only here, "little children" (*teknia*). John will use the term seven times in his first letter. For him it became the title of his followers. Once more Jesus is warning that he will not be with them much longer. For the fifth time he tells them that they cannot follow him to the place he is about to go (Jn 7:34; 8:21, 22; 13:33).

The statement in verse 34 opens a section fully four chapters long. Here Jesus will give his disciples their last instructions. Again and again he will return to the theme of love. Here, in verse 34, he mentions it for the very first time.

Previously the only command Jesus had referred to was the one he has received from his Father (Jn 10:18; 12:49-50). Now he gives his disciples a new commandment of his own. The question, "Which is the greatest commandment?" reverberates throughout the Gospels (Mt 5:43; 19:19; 22:39; Mk 12:31, 33; Lk 10:27). John has omitted all of these discussions, providing instead Jesus' new commandment to love each other. He commands that they love as he has loved them, his clothes still wet from having just washed their feet. It is the single defining mark of his disciples. It is the one nonnegotiable in following Jesus. It was the most single important thing Jesus had said this evening, and Peter has completely missed the point. He is still stuck on what Jesus said in verse 33 about the fact that they cannot go where he is about to go.

"Where are you going, Lord?" Peter asks in verse 36. Has Peter perceived all of the insinuations of death and decided that Jesus was really talking about death as the place they could not follow? Peter looks Jesus straight in the eye, meaning it with every fiber of his being, and says that he will lay down his life for Jesus. This is not the buffoon of so many misrepresentations. The man who spoke these words will indeed die one

day for his friend Jesus. But for now, it is not the point. Once more Jesus
wants to focus on what God intends to do and not what anyone of them
is doing. I hear just a hint of impatience in Jesus' voice, a note of frustration, having been pulled off the point once again.

"Will you really?" he asks. I can imagine Jesus regretting it the moment the words left his lips. Peter needs to hear these words, as painful
as they might be to hear. He will disown Jesus three times.

JOHN 14

THE PERFECT COMFORT

[1]"Your heart must not be troubled. Believe in God; believe also in Me. [2]In My Father's house are many dwelling places; if not, I would have told you. I am going away to prepare a place for you. [3]If I go away and prepare a place for you, I will come back and receive you to Myself, so that where I am you may be also. [4]You know the way to where I am going."

[5]"Lord," Thomas said, "we don't know where You're going. How can we know the way?"

[6]Jesus told him, "I am the way, the truth, and the life. No one comes to the Father except through Me.

[7]"If you know Me, you will also know My Father. From now on you do know Him and have seen Him."

[8]"Lord," said Philip, "show us the Father, and that's enough for us."

[9]Jesus said to him, "Have I been among you all this time without your knowing Me, Philip? The one who has seen Me has seen the Father. How can you say, 'Show us the Father'? [10]Don't you believe that I am in the Father and the Father is in Me? The words I speak to you I do not speak on My own. The Father who lives in Me does His works. [11]Believe Me that I am in the Father and the Father is in Me. Otherwise, believe because of the works themselves.

[12]"I assure you: The one who believes in Me will also do the works that I do. And he will do even greater works than these, because I am going to the Father. [13]Whatever you ask in My name, I will do it so that the Father may be glorified in the Son. [14]If you ask Me anything in My name, I will do it."

With chapter 14 Jesus' farewell discourse begins in earnest. At the end of the chapter they will leave the upper room. For three more chapters Jesus will speak with the disciples on the way to Gethsemane. With chapter 18 the arrest occurs and the final series of events leading to the cross begins.

As you read chapter 14, try to imagine the tone of the conversation just after Jesus has washed the disciples' feet. In the previous chapter Jesus had spoken some troubling things: he will be betrayed, he's going to a place where they cannot follow, and Peter would disown him three times.

In that context the opening statement of chapter 14 comes into focus.

"Do not let your hearts be troubled," says Jesus, who has just spoken many troubling things to them. While he might soon be going to a place where they cannot follow, he is also going to prepare a place for each one of them to stay. While they cannot follow him, he promises in verse 3 to come back and take them to be with him. You can almost sense the tension and anxiety in the room easing with those comforting words.

In John 14 Jesus is interrupted three times, first by Thomas in verse 5, next by Philip in verse 8 and finally by the other Judas in verse 22. With each interruption Jesus will posit himself as the answer to the question. The three exchanges are less like the motif of misunderstanding and have more the tone of a reasonable exchange. The disciples are beginning to know that they don't know.

Jesus had said in verse 4 that they knew the way to the place he was going. Thomas honestly engages: they don't know where so how could they know the way? Jesus points to himself. He is the way, and the truth and the life. Jesus has alluded to the fact that he is the truth (Jn 8:32; see Jn 1:14, 17) and the life (Jn 5:26; 6:35; 11:25; see Jn 1:4), but this is the only time he refers to himself as the way.

In response to Jesus' statement in verse 7—that to know him is to know the Father, that in knowing him they have known and seen the Father—Philip effects the second interruption. If Jesus will simply show them the Father, they will be satisfied. Once again, it is a reasonable request, which Jesus chooses to ignore.

Jesus' exclusive claim as the only way to the Father is not only a Johannine theme. Matthew 11:27 echoes the claim: "No one knows the Son except the Father, and no one knows the Father except the Son and anyone to whom the Son desires to reveal Him." In the preaching of Peter in Acts 4:12 we read: "There is salvation in no one else, for there is no other name under heaven given to people, and we must be saved by it."

Jesus' response to Philip sounds somewhat tense. Doesn't Philip know him, even after such a long time together? How can Philip ask such a thing? The Father is alive in Jesus, speaking through him, doing his work.

Jesus repeats it for the sixth time in verse 11. He is in the Father, and the Father is in him. Everything is rooted in their oneness: Jesus' words and works, and the disciples' ability to know God and to eventually perform even greater works.

ANOTHER COMFORTER

[15]*"If you love Me, you will keep My commands.* [16]*And I will ask the Father, and He will give you another Counselor to be with you forever.* [17]*He is the Spirit of truth. The world is unable to receive Him because it doesn't see Him or know Him. But you do know Him, because He remains with you and will be in you.* [18]*I will not leave you as orphans; I am coming to you.*

[19]*"In a little while the world will see Me no longer, but you will see Me. Because I live, you will live too.* [20]*In that day you will know that I am in My Father, you are in Me, and I am in you.* [21]*The one who has My commands and keeps them is the one who loves Me. And the one who loves Me will be loved by My Father. I also will love him and will reveal Myself to him."*

[22]*Judas (not Iscariot) said to Him, "Lord, how is it You're going to reveal Yourself to us and not to the world?"*

[23]*Jesus answered, "If anyone loves Me, he will keep My word. My Father will love him, and We will come to him and make Our home with him.* [24]*The one who doesn't love Me will not keep My words. The word that you hear is not Mine but is from the Father who sent Me.*

[25]*"I have spoken these things to you while I remain with you.* [26]*But the Counselor, the Holy Spirit—the Father will send Him in My name—will teach you all things and remind you of everything I have told you.*

[27]*"Peace I leave with you. My peace I give to you. I do not give to you as the world gives. Your heart must not be troubled or fearful.* [28]*You have heard Me tell you, 'I am going away and I am coming to you.' If you loved Me, you would have rejoiced that I am going to the Father, because the Father is greater than I.* [29]*I have told you now before it happens so that when it does happen you may believe.* [30]*I will not talk with you much longer, because the ruler of the world is coming. He has no power over Me.* [31]*On the contrary, I am going away so that the world may know that I love the Father. Just as the Father commanded Me, so I do.*

"Get up; let's leave this place."

*W*ith that remarkable promise in verse 12 that the disciples will do even greater works, Jesus begins a lengthy discussion (vv. 15-31) on the bond between love and obedience.

- If you love me you will keep my commandments. (v. 15)
- The one who . . . keeps my commands is the one who loves me. (v. 21)
- If anyone loves me he will keep my word. (v. 23)
- The one who doesn't love me will not keep my words. (v. 24)
- I love the father, just as the father commanded me, so I do. (v. 31)

Next, in light of their discomfort Jesus promises to send the Comforter (Counselor). The Greek word *parakletos* is a compound word: *para*, "beside"; *kaleo*, "to call." Literally the term means "the one who is called alongside." There are two different ways of understanding the term. The first is legal. The person who "stands beside you" in court is thus a counselor or advocate (NIV 2011). The other shade of meaning connotes someone who comes alongside you in sorrow to comfort you, thus a comforter. The HCSB chose "Counselor." In light of the context of the troubled hearts of the disciples and of all the discomforting things Jesus had said about leaving and betrayal, I believe *Comforter* makes more sense at first. Notice that Jesus says "another Comforter." He is the original.

- He is the Spirit of truth, as Jesus is the truth.
- The world will not accept him even as it has not accepted Jesus.
- He will live in the disciples as the Father lives in Jesus.
- Jesus will not leave them as orphans, that is "comfortless." (KJV)

He will come to them. Jesus and the Spirit are one, as he and the Father are one. Soon the disciples will realize that Jesus is in the Father, that they are in him and he in them (v. 20).

The third interruption comes from the other Judas (see Lk 6:16; Acts 1:13). In verse 21 Jesus had promised that the person who loved him would be loved by both the Father and Jesus, and Jesus would show himself to them. Judas wonders out loud why Jesus is showing himself to his disciples (the ones who love him) and not to the whole world. It is a legitimate question, which Jesus ignores.

Jesus returns to the ideas of love and obedience. Those who love him will obey. In turn the Father will love them, come to them and together Jesus and the Father will make their home with them. Verses 25-31 contain Jesus' summing up after the meal and preparing to move out into the night toward Gethsemane. He focuses on hearing and remembering. He has spoken of them while he was with them, but the Comforter, the Holy Spirit, will be sent to teach and remind them of all the things Jesus had said.

Jesus closes this portion of the discourse with words about love. If they loved him, they would be glad that he was returning to the Father. He reminds them once more that they do not have much longer together. Echoing the connections between love and obedience, Jesus looks ahead to the cross, saying that the world must learn that he loves the Father and does exactly what the Father has commanded him. On the cross Jesus will demonstrate his love for the Father by his radical obedience.

Judas is, at this very moment, going to the high priest. The wheels have been set in motion. There is not much time. It is a short walk from the city, across the Kidron Valley to Gethsemane.

"Come now, let us leave," Jesus says.

JOHN 15

THE WALK

15:1–27

THE WALK

[1]"I am the true vine, and My Father is the vineyard keeper. [2]Every branch in Me that does not produce fruit He removes, and He prunes every branch that produces fruit so that it will produce more fruit. [3]You are already clean because of the word I have spoken to you. [4]Remain in Me, and I in you. Just as a branch is unable to produce fruit by itself unless it remains on the vine, so neither can you unless you remain in Me.

[5]"I am the vine; you are the branches. The one who remains in Me and I in him produces much fruit, because you can do nothing without Me. [6]If anyone does not remain in Me, he is thrown aside like a branch and he withers. They gather them, throw them into the fire, and they are burned. [7]If you remain in Me and My words remain in you, ask whatever you want and it will be done for you. [8]My Father is glorified by this: that you produce much fruit and prove to be My disciples.

[9]"As the Father has loved Me, I have also loved you. Remain in My love. [10]If you keep My commands you will remain in My love, just as I have kept My Father's commands and remain in His love.

[11]"I have spoken these things to you so that My joy may be in you and your joy may be complete. [12]This is My command: Love one another as I have loved you. [13]No one has greater love than this, that someone would lay down his life for his friends. [14]You are My friends if you do what I command you. [15]I do not call you slaves anymore, because a slave doesn't know what his master is doing. I have called you friends, because I have made known to you everything I have heard from My Father. [16]You did not choose Me, but I chose you. I appointed you that you should go out and produce fruit and that your fruit should remain, so that whatever you ask the Father in My name, He will give you. [17]This is what I command you: Love one another.

[18]"If the world hates you, understand that it hated Me before it hated you. [19]If you were of the world, the world would love you as its own. However, because you are not of the world, but I have chosen you out of it, the world hates you. [20]Remember the word I spoke to you: 'A slave is not greater than his master.' If they persecuted Me, they will also persecute you. If they kept My word, they will also keep yours. [21]But they will do all these things to you on account of My name, because they don't know the One who sent Me. [22]If I had not come and spoken to them, they would not have sin. Now they have

no excuse for their sin. ²³The one who hates Me also hates My Father. ²⁴If I had not done the works among them that no one else has done, they would not have sin. Now they have seen and hated both Me and My Father. ²⁵But this happened so that the statement written in their scripture might be fulfilled: They hated Me for no reason.

²⁶"When the Counselor comes, the One I will send to you from the Father—the Spirit of truth who proceeds from the Father—He will testify about Me. ²⁷You also will testify, because you have been with Me from the beginning."

Chapters 15–17 contain Jesus' final intimate words to his disciples as they made their way to the Garden of Gethsemane. Occasionally the passage will represent the disjointedness of a walk. There must have been some urgency in Jesus' voice. This was not a leisurely stroll. Jesus will double back, repeating words and images he has used throughout his ministry. He will talk about love and fruit bearing. He will warn his disciples of the persecution that is in store for them in the near future. He will return to the topic of the Holy Spirit and explain in more detail the Spirit's work. And he will pray—for himself, for his disciples and even for us, all those in the future who will believe through the message of the disciples. These chapters should be read as a whole, in one sitting. This is the only way to develop an understanding of the flow of the discourse and to become aware of the many significant repetitions.

The chapter begins with Jesus' final "I am" saying. As they are making their way out of the city, there is a chance they passed the temple complex. One of its many ornaments was a sculpted vine decorating one of the walls. Perhaps Jesus used it as an example. Notice that he cannot say that he is the vine without at the same time including his Father in the image as the gardener. Even as Jesus had been the true light and the true bread, so he is also the true vine, the genuine reality of which all other references in the Old Testament were only shadows (Ps 80:8-18; Is 5:1-7; Jer 2:21; Ezek 15; Hos 10:1). Three times in verse 4 Jesus repeats the idea of remaining in him, that is, staying attached to the true vine for nourishment. Otherwise his disciples will never be able to bear fruit.

Fruit bearing is the other concept that is repeated the most, five more times in this chapter. Jesus concludes the vine section of the discussion by reminding his disciples once again that the purpose of bearing fruit is to bring glory to the Father (see Jn 14:13).

In verses 9-17 Jesus returns again to the idea of the connection between love and obedience. As the disciples were to remain in the vine, now Jesus begins by saying they must remain in his love. In verse 10 he connects once more the idea of obedience to his commands and remaining in his love. Jesus, always our exemplar, obeyed his Father's commands and remained in his love. Now, as they make their way toward the garden, he tells them to do the same.

Verses 12-13 are another echo, another repetition of something he said earlier in John 13:34. There he called it his "new commandment." Here he simply says his command is this: "love one other as I have loved you." Don't forget that only an hour or so ago he had demonstrated the full extent of his love by washing their feet. That moment is still very clear in the disciples' minds and hearts. (This is another example of the importance of reading large blocks for the sake of flow and continuity.)

From a discussion of obedience and love, Jesus moves to a discourse on hate (vv. 18-25). He is trying to give the disciples a much-needed dose of perspective. Again, he is the exemplar. If the world hates the disciples, remember that it hated Jesus first. The Eleven will not be the last of Jesus' followers to struggle with understanding the hatred of the world and why it is directed against them simply because they belong to Jesus. It is a word his followers all over the world still need to hear. More disciples of Jesus are dying now than at any time in the history of the church.

Jesus reminds them of something he said earlier: that no servant is greater than his or her master (Jn 13:16). (Once again notice how often Jesus is repeating himself.) The principle applies to persecution as well. If the master is persecuted, then his servants should not be surprised when persecution comes to them.

Verse 23 begins to reflect the disjointedness of a walk. Jesus, still talking about the hatred of the world, says that those who hate him are in reality hating the Father. The idea of his oneness with the Father has been a steady theme for the past several chapters. It is as if Jesus is speaking encouragement to himself as much as to the disciples. Jesus had spoken to them (v. 22) and had done miracles among them (v. 24). The response of the world is hatred. All the while, keep in mind that Jesus is walking headlong into the storm of the world's hatred. He even finds justification for it in their "law" (Scripture). In a very Johannine way Jesus illustrates it with a psalm: "They hated me without reason" (Ps 35:19; 69:4).

In verse 26 Jesus' mind turns back to the Comforter, for if anyone ever needed comfort, Jesus and his disciples do at this moment. He is coming from the Father. He will testify, as they also must testify, because they have been with him from "the beginning" (Jn 1:1).

JOHN 16

A RADICAL REDEFINITION

16:1–16

A MOVEMENT AWAY
FROM MISUNDERSTANDING

16:17–33

A RADICAL REDEFINITION

[1]"I have told you these things to keep you from stumbling. [2]They will ban you from the synagogues. In fact, a time is coming when anyone who kills you will think he is offering service to God. [3]They will do these things because they haven't known the Father or Me. [4]But I have told you these things so that when their time comes you may remember I told them to you. I didn't tell you these things from the beginning, because I was with you.

[5]"But now I am going away to Him who sent Me, and not one of you asks Me, 'Where are You going?' [6]Yet, because I have spoken these things to you, sorrow has filled your heart. [7]Nevertheless, I am telling you the truth. It is for your benefit that I go away, because if I don't go away the Counselor will not come to you. If I go, I will send Him to you. [8]When He comes, He will convict the world about sin, righteousness, and judgment: [9]About sin, because they do not believe in Me; [10]about righteousness, because I am going to the Father and you will no longer see Me; [11]and about judgment because the ruler of this world has been judged.

[12]"I still have many things to tell you, but you can't bear them now. [13]When the Spirit of truth comes, He will guide you into all the truth. For He will not speak on His own, but He will speak whatever He hears. He will also declare to you what is to come. [14]He will glorify Me, because He will take from what is Mine and declare it to you. [15]Everything the Father has is Mine. This is why I told you that He takes from what is Mine and will declare it to you.

[16]"A little while and you will no longer see Me; again a little while and you will see Me."

*A*s they approach Gethsemane and all that lies waiting for him there, Jesus speaks a word of encouragement that would have resonated with the first readers of John's Gospel in Ephesus as much as it did that evening with the Eleven. He has been trying to inoculate them from stumbling by telling them beforehand that persecution is coming. The word for stumbling, *skandalizo*, is an important theme in the New Testament's presentation of Jesus as the "stone that causes people to stumble and the rock that makes them fall" (NIV), first prophesied in Isaiah 8:14 (see Mt 21:42; Rom 9:33; 1 Pet 2:8). He warns them of the ban, which has already been pronounced on Jesus, being extended to them in the future (see also Jn 9:22; 12:42). This does not simply mean being kicked out of the synagogue but being expelled from Jewish life and community. What's more, Jesus warns, others will believe they are serving God by killing the disciples. Saul of Tarsus would be one of the first persecutors. Jesus reasserts that he is telling them now so that when it happens they will remember. They will not experience any persecution that Jesus did not experience himself. He has waited until now to tell them, the end of their time together, because before he was with them.

In verses 5-7 Jesus repeats the notion that he is leaving, but now he connects his departure to the coming of the Holy Spirit, who cannot come until Jesus leaves. In verses 8-11 he offers three new promises about the work of the Spirit. In these verses *parakletos* might be alternately translated "Counselor," for the setting sounds more like a courtroom. When the Spirit comes he will radically redefine three of the most basic notions of spirituality: sin, righteousness, and judgment. In each case the Spirit will reveal that the world is fundamentally wrong in its understanding of all three.

The world is wrong about sin because according to the new definition sin is not believing in Jesus. Before, the opposite of sin was righteousness. Now the opposite of sin is faith in Jesus.

The world is wrong about righteousness because they condemn Jesus. But his righteousness will be demonstrated by his returning to the Father. Before the coming of Jesus, righteousness was based on human performance. Now it is a result of right relationship with the Father, which only comes through Jesus.

Finally, the world is wrong about judgment, because Jesus' sacrificial death on the cross will result in the condemnation of Satan, the prince of this world. As they stand jeering before the cross, the Jews will wrongly believe that Jesus' death is justified because of their condemnation of him. They could never have dreamed that his death was atoning for the world's sin.

There is much more to say, but time is running short. Besides, when the Spirit comes, he will speak to the disciples about all these things (v. 13). In a matter of hours ("a little while") Jesus will be taken from them. Three days later they will see him once more (v. 16).

A MOVEMENT AWAY FROM MISUNDERSTANDING

[17]Therefore some of His disciples said to one another, "What is this He tells us: 'A little while and you will not see Me; again a little while and you will see Me'; and, 'because I am going to the Father'?" [18]They said, "What is this He is saying, 'A little while'? We don't know what He's talking about!"

[19]Jesus knew they wanted to question Him, so He said to them, "Are you asking one another about what I said, 'A little while and you will not see Me; again a little while and you will see Me'?

[20]"I assure you: You will weep and wail, but the world will rejoice. You will become sorrowful, but your sorrow will turn to joy. [21]When a woman is in labor she has pain because her time has come. But when she has given birth to a child, she no longer remembers the suffering because of the joy that a person has been born into the world. [22]So you also have sorrow now. But I will see you again. Your hearts will rejoice, and no one will rob you of your joy. [23]In that day you will not ask Me anything.

"I assure you: Anything you ask the Father in My name, He will give you. [24]Until now you have asked for nothing in My name. Ask and you will receive, so that your joy may be complete.

[25]"I have spoken these things to you in figures of speech. A time is coming when I will no longer speak to you in figures, but I will tell you plainly about the Father. [26]In that day you will ask in My name. I am not telling you that I will make requests to the Father on your behalf. [27]For the Father Himself loves you, because you have loved Me and have believed that I came from God. [28]I came from the Father and have come into the world. Again, I am leaving the world and going to the Father."

[29]"Ah!" His disciples said. "Now You're speaking plainly and not using any figurative language. [30]Now we know that You know everything and don't need anyone to question You. By this we believe that You came from God."

[31]Jesus responded to them, "Do you now believe? [32]Look: An hour is coming, and has come, when each of you will be scattered to his own home, and you will leave Me alone. Yet I am not alone, because the Father is with Me. [33]I have told you these things so that in Me you may have peace. You will have suffering in this world. Be courageous! I have conquered the world."

*I*n verses 17-18 you might be tempted to see yet another example of John's favorite theme, the motif of misunderstanding. Yes, Jesus has just said something spiritual, but listen more closely to the response of the Eleven. They are not making a ludicrous proposal as individuals have in the past (see Jn 7:35; 8:22). Even though the disciples do not have the answer, they are moving from the dimwittedness they have demonstrated all along. Listen to their response. First, they quote Jesus' words precisely, indicating they were actually listening. The second sentence of verse 18 contains the genuine breakthrough. They confess that they don't understand what Jesus is talking about. For the first time they actually know that they don't know (see Jn 12:16; Lk 24:45)!

Jesus responds to their question in verses 19-22. He paints a picture of the next few days. The world will celebrate Jesus' death while the disciples weep and mourn. But the radical reversal associated with Jesus' appearing will win the day. Using the metaphor of a woman in the pains of childbirth, Jesus draws once more from an image found in the prophets (Is 21:3; 26:17; Hos 13:13; Mic 4:9-10). A woman giving birth to a child experiences the same radical reversal from pain to overwhelming joy. That joy will be theirs when they see Jesus alive again, and no one will be able to rob them of that joy—ever.

Verse 23 would make a good paragraph break. Here Jesus introduces a new privilege to the Eleven: the ability to ask in Jesus' name. He encourages them from now on to go straight to the Father, as he will go straight to the Father in prayer in chapter 17. He completes the thought by returning once again to joy. The new privilege of asking in Jesus' name is tied to their joy (see Jn 15:11).

Jesus is quickly coming to the end of his long final discourse with the Eleven. In chapter 17 he will go to prayer. He comes to a conclusion by promising that the time is rapidly approaching when he will no longer speak in figures of speech but will speak to them openly about the Father. They will speak to the Father directly in Jesus' name, and the Father, who loves them, will hear. Verse 28 is Jesus' response to his own question, a question the disciples had failed to ask back in verse 5, "Where are you going?" He came from the Father. Now he is leaving and returning to the Father. Before they did not understand (v. 17). Finally, it becomes clear with Jesus' straightforward answer. He is not speaking in figures of speech, they respond. They conclude at last that Jesus is from God.

Jesus' opening phrase in verse 31 can be translated as either a statement or a question. Once you understand the choices, you can make as good a determination as anyone. He is either commending their perception and affirming the reality of their belief or he is still asking if they really do believe given the fact that in a few verses they are going to abandon him. Verse 33 is the final statement of his long discourse, and it is the perfect conclusion not simply of all he has said for the last four chapters but of all he has expressed to them over the last three years. In him they will have peace, shalom. The world will offer nothing but pain and disappointment. His final words before he turns to the Father in prayer are spoken as much to you and me as to the Eleven: "Be courageous! I have conquered the world."

JOHN 17

GLORIFY YOUR SON

¹Jesus spoke these things, looked up to heaven, and said:
Father,
the hour has come.
Glorify Your Son
so that the Son may glorify You,
²for You gave Him authority
over all flesh;
so He may give eternal life
to all You have given Him.
³This is eternal life:
that they may know You, the only true God,
and the One You have sent—Jesus Christ.
⁴I have glorified You on the earth
by completing the work You gave Me to do.
⁵Now, Father, glorify Me in Your presence
with that glory I had with You
before the world existed.

*I*f you really want to get to know someone, listen to them pray. Chapter 17 is the longest and most personal prayer of Jesus in the New Testament. It reveals the intimacy of the relationship he had with the Father. Again, Jesus repeats himself. His predominant themes are glory and oneness.

We cannot say for certain whether Jesus' consistent posture in prayer was to "look up to heaven," but this is not the only time we see him praying like this. When he feeds the five thousand, Matthew, Mark and Luke all mention that Jesus was looking up as he prayed (Mt 14:19; Mk 6:41; Lk 9:16). Mark adds one other instance, when Jesus healed the deaf man in Mark 7:34. There too he looked up to heaven when he cried out "Be opened!"

As he approaches the darkness of Gethsemane and all that awaits him there, Jesus' prayer focuses on glory. He asks that the Father would glorify him so that he might glorify the Father. He affirms in verse 4 that he has brought God glory by completing the work he was given. In verse 5 he asks the Father again to glorify him with the glory he had known before the creation of the world (see Prov 8:23). The distinction between giving and receiving glory practically disappears in the context of the mutual love between Jesus and the Father.

PROTECT AND SANCTIFY THE ELEVEN

⁶I have revealed Your name
to the men You gave Me from the world.
They were Yours, You gave them to Me,
and they have kept Your word.
⁷Now they know that all things
You have given to Me are from You,
⁸because the words that You gave Me,
I have given them.
They have received them
and have known for certain
that I came from You.
They have believed that You sent Me.
⁹I pray for them.
I am not praying for the world
but for those You have given Me,
because they are Yours.
¹⁰Everything I have is Yours,
and everything You have is Mine,
and I have been glorified in them.
¹¹I am no longer in the world,
but they are in the world,
and I am coming to You.
Holy Father,
protect them by Your name
that You have given Me,
so that they may be one as We are one.
¹²While I was with them,
I was protecting them by Your name
that You have given Me.

I guarded them and not one of them is lost,
except the son of destruction,
so that the Scripture may be fulfilled.
¹³Now I am coming to You,
and I speak these things in the world
so that they may have My joy completed in them.
¹⁴I have given them Your word.
The world hated them
because they are not of the world,
as I am not of the world.
¹⁵I am not praying
that You take them out of the world
but that You protect them from the evil one.
¹⁶They are not of the world,
as I am not of the world.
¹⁷Sanctify them by the truth;
Your word is truth.
¹⁸As You sent Me into the world,
I also have sent them into the world.
¹⁹I sanctify Myself for them,
so they also may be sanctified by the truth.

$\mathcal{W}$ ith the mountain of suffering and separation from the Father that lies before him, Jesus still spends the majority of this prayer asking for protection and unity for the Eleven and for all who would follow him based on their message.

His statement in verse 7, "Now they know," might indicate that his opening words in John 16:31 were indeed an affirmation that they genuinely believed. Also in verse 8 he states that they "have known for certain." Again, perhaps the Eleven have grasped more than we have given them credit for in the past.

In verses 9-12 Jesus petitions the Father for protection for the Eleven. He specifies that he is not praying for the world (*kosmos*). The term *world* in John almost always represents the fallen world that is at odds with God's will (Jn 1:10; 3:19; 7:7; 8:23; 12:31; 14:17, 27, 30; 15:18; 16:11, 33; 18:36). Even the notion of protection is tied to the theme of glory in verse 10. Glory has come to Jesus through the disciples, whom he is asking the Father to protect. Jesus has protected them up until now and kept them safe by the Father's name (v. 12). But now that he is leaving the world, he places the Eleven, and you and me, in the Father's loving protection.

In the second part of verse 12 Judas appears as the "son of perishing" (destruction). There is a play on words that none of the popular translations capture. Literally Jesus says, "None has perished except the son of perishing." The same term is used in 2 Thessalonians 2:3 in referring to the antichrist.

Verse 13 hints at the fact that Jesus is speaking his prayer out loud, specifically so the disciples can hear his words and receive joy. Jesus makes this clear when he prays for the raising of Lazarus in John 11:41-42. He states that he is saying these things for the benefit of the listeners, since he knows the Father always listens.

In verses 14-19 Jesus asks that the Eleven be sanctified or set apart. According to his prayer, what sets the disciples apart is the truth and the word that is truth. Since they are being sent out into a world that is hostile to the truth, the Father must protect and sanctify them. Note that Jesus does not ask that the disciples be taken out of the world but that they be set apart from the world.

LET THEM BE ONE

20I pray not only for these,
but also for those who believe in Me
through their message.
21May they all be one,
as You, Father, are in Me and I am in You.
May they also be one in Us,
so the world may believe You sent Me.
22I have given them the glory You have given Me.
May they be one as We are one.
23I am in them and You are in Me.

> *May they be made completely one,*
> *so the world may know You have sent Me*
> *and have loved them as You have loved Me.*
> ²⁴*Father,*
> *I desire those You have given Me*
> *to be with Me where I am.*
> *Then they will see My glory,*
> *which You have given Me*
> *because You loved Me before the world's foundation.*
> ²⁵*Righteous Father!*
> *The world has not known You.*
> *However, I have known You,*
> *and these have known that You sent Me.*
> ²⁶*I made Your name known to them*
> *and will make it known,*
> *so the love You have loved Me with*
> *may be in them and I may be in them.*

*I*t is remarkable enough that Jesus, in the midst of his sorrow, the weight of which he says is about to kill him (Mt 26:38), looks into the future and prays for his future followers—for you and me! His principal request is for oneness or unity. Our unity is a reflection of the unity that had always existed between Jesus and the Father.

Finally, Jesus returns to the idea of glory. He wants his future followers to see his glory, a glory that comes from the love that Father has always had, since before the creation of the world. Here the word for love is *agape*.

Jesus closes his prayer by referring to God in words he has never used until this moment: Righteous Father. Listen to the pathos in his voice as he affirms, "I know you." In a matter of hours he will scream from the cross, "Why have You forsaken Me?" (Mt 27:46; Mk 15:34).

JOHN 18

THE ARREST

¹*After Jesus had said these things, He went out with His disciples across the Kidron Valley, where there was a garden, and He and His disciples went into it. ²Judas, who betrayed Him, also knew the place, because Jesus often met there with His disciples. ³So Judas took a company of soldiers and some temple police from the chief priests and the Pharisees and came there with lanterns, torches, and weapons.*

⁴*Then Jesus, knowing everything that was about to happen to Him, went out and said to them, "Who is it you're looking for?"*

⁵*"Jesus the Nazarene," they answered.*

"I am He," Jesus told them.

Judas, who betrayed Him, was also standing with them. ⁶When He told them, "I am He," they stepped back and fell to the ground.

⁷*Then He asked them again, "Who is it you're looking for?"*

"Jesus the Nazarene," they said.

⁸*"I told you I am He," Jesus replied. "So if you're looking for Me, let these men go." ⁹This was to fulfill the words He had said: "I have not lost one of those You have given Me."*

¹⁰*Then Simon Peter, who had a sword, drew it, struck the high priest's slave, and cut off his right ear. (The slave's name was Malchus.)*

¹¹*At that, Jesus said to Peter, "Sheathe your sword! Am I not to drink the cup the Father has given Me?"*

*T*he time for prayer is over. Jesus has said all that he needs to say to the Eleven, and so they make their way across the Kidron Valley, the large ravine that lies between the walls of Jerusalem and the Garden of Gethsemane. In Jesus' day this area was more an industrial complex than the simple gardens that exists there today. Historically, David had crossed the valley in 2 Samuel 15:23 as he was fleeing from his son Absalom. Ezekiel had seen the valley in one of his visions (Ezek 47:1-5).

John omits Jesus' prayer in the garden and the story of him returning three times to check on Peter, James and John (Mt 26:36-46; Mk 14:32-

42; Lk 22:40-46). John has substituted the earlier "high priestly" prayer of Jesus in chapter 17.

Immediately the action shifts to Judas, who knew that Jesus would be here. He appears with a "company" of guards. John omits the detail of Judas's kiss. Perhaps he could not bring himself to recount it again. The word John uses to describe the group that Judas is leading is a technical military term for cohort (*speira*). Matthew and Mark both use the term (Mt 27:27; Mk 15:16). Luke uses it to refer to both the Italian cohort (Acts 10:1) and the Augustan cohort (Acts 27:1). The word implies that these are Roman soldiers from the Antonia Fortress. There could have been as many as two hundred to six hundred in a cohort. There is wide disagreement among scholars on this detail. Some do not think John is using the term literally but rather simply to describe a group of temple guards. Apart from the question whether they are Roman or simply temple guards, it is safe to say that it is a much larger contingent than is usually portrayed either in art or in our imaginations. John provides the detail that they are heavily armed and are carrying weapons, lanterns and torches. They are expecting a fight as well as an extended search, despite the fact that there is a full Passover moon in the sky. There are chief priests, who are Sadducees, and members of the Pharisees, two groups that would normally never work together, but now they have their mutual hatred of Jesus as a bond.

John knows that Jesus knew exactly what was going to happen, because all along the way to Jerusalem he had told the disciples about it in ever-increasing detail. He straightforwardly walks up to the armed group and asks who they seek. Their simple reply: "Jesus of Nazareth" (v. 5).

There are two possibilities of understanding Jesus' response. He answers *ego eimi*, which can simply be translated either "I am he" or "I AM," the divine and unspeakable name of God (Ex 3:14). The response of the soldiers can be interpreted in two different ways as well. If Jesus merely said, "I am he," their response could be a military one, best described as falling back in anticipation of an ambush. They were obviously prepared for a search and a struggle. They never expected the object of their search to calmly walk right up to them.

John 18   185

If, on the other hand, Jesus spoke the name of God, the reference to everyone falling to the ground is the prescribed response at hearing the unspeakable name spoken. I believe that perhaps we are seeing both responses. The Roman soldiers "fall back" in military style in expectation of an ambush. The Jewish leaders fall down at hearing the divine name.

In verse 7 Jesus speaks calmly to both groups cowering on the ground. Once more he asks them who they are looking for. This scene would be comic if it were not so tragic. Jesus repeats that he is the person they are looking for and asks that his men be let go. This is the first example of his words being fulfilled. In John 6:39 he had said that it was the Father's will that he would not lose a single one of those who had been entrusted to him.

Matthew and Mark tell us at this time some of the soldiers move forward to take hold of Jesus. Luke tells the story from the standpoint of the disciples and says that at this moment they saw what was about to happen to Jesus (Lk 22:49). John leaves out those details and simply says that Peter drew his sword and took a swipe at the high priest's servant, cutting off his ear. John, who from this point in the story will demonstrate an increasing amount of local knowledge, knows the servant's name was Malchus. Clement of Alexandria explains John's inside information about Jerusalem had come from the fact that John's father, Zebedee, sold fish in the city.

Some scholars have said that this was Peter's deliberate attempt to disfigure Malchus so that he would be disqualified from serving in the temple. Behind this theory is a story from Josephus. Antigonus, the final priest-king of the Hasmonean dynasty (40–37 B.C.), opposed a high priest who had been placed in office by the Parthians and so bit off one of his ears so that he would be disqualified from serving in the temple.[1] While it is based on firm historical background, I hardly think it mattered to Peter whether the high priest's servant could serve in the temple or not. He was not aiming for his ear but rather his throat. Malchus turns his head at the last moment and only loses an earlobe. Jesus steps into the confusion, telling Peter to put his sword away. John omits the subtle healing of Malchus (Lk 22:51).

PETER'S FIRST DENIALS

[12]Then the company of soldiers, the commander, and the Jewish temple police arrested Jesus and tied Him up. [13]First they led Him to Annas, for he was the father-in-law of Caiaphas, who was high priest that year. [14]Caiaphas was the one who had advised the Jews that it was advantageous that one man should die for the people.

[15]Meanwhile, Simon Peter was following Jesus, as was another disciple. That disciple was an acquaintance of the high priest; so he went with Jesus into the high priest's courtyard. [16]But Peter remained standing outside by the door. So the other disciple, the one known to the high priest, went out and spoke to the girl who was the doorkeeper and brought Peter in.

[17]Then the slave girl who was the doorkeeper said to Peter, "You aren't one of this man's disciples too, are you?"

"I am not!" he said. [18]Now the slaves and the temple police had made a charcoal fire, because it was cold. They were standing there warming themselves, and Peter was standing with them, warming himself.

Only John's Gospel tells of the first phase of Jesus' arrest, that he was held at the house of Annas, the father-in-law of Caiaphas, while the Sanhedrin was being summoned. Annas was the most powerful high priest of first-century Jerusalem. Five of his sons; Caiaphas, his son-in-law; and even one of his grandsons served as high priest from A.D. 16 to 66.[2] Even though he is not in office at this point, he still may be considered the most influential person in Jerusalem. John will return to the scene once more in verse 19.

In verses 15-18 John gives the account of the first of Peter's three denials. The "other disciple" who is following along with Peter is almost certainly John. Again, we see evidence of his local knowledge. He is known to the servant girl who minds the gate and is allowed into the courtyard, along with Jesus. John is present as an acknowledged follower of Jesus. This is an important detail if we are to fully understand the background of Peter's denials. Peter, at first, is forced to wait outside until, in verse 16, John speaks to the slave girl at the gate, who allows Peter to be admitted.

Listen closely to what she says. "You aren't one of this man's disciples too, are you?" She has in mind John, who apparently is not afraid that everyone there knows he is one of Jesus' followers.

Caught off-guard, Peter replies that he is not a follower of Jesus—his first denial. His betrayal wins him a place close to the fire with the slaves and the officials.

JESUS AND ANNAS

[19] The high priest questioned Jesus about His disciples and about His teaching. [20] "I have spoken openly to the world," Jesus answered him. "I have always taught in the synagogue and in the temple complex, where all the Jews congregate, and I haven't spoken anything in secret. [21] Why do you question Me? Question those who heard what I told them. Look, they know what I said."

[22] When He had said these things, one of the temple police standing by slapped Jesus, saying, "Is this the way you answer the high priest?"

[23] "If I have spoken wrongly," Jesus answered him, "give evidence about the wrong; but if rightly, why do you hit Me?"

[24] Then Annas sent Him bound to Caiaphas the high priest.

*V*erses 19-24 provide an account of Jesus' preliminary questioning before Annas, whom John also refers to as the high priest. This is the first step of the Jewish trial. Step two will be Jesus' interrogation before Caiaphas at an illegal meeting of the Sanhedrin in the middle of the night (Mt 26:57). John chooses to omit that section of the trial. The third and final part of the Jewish trial will be the early morning meeting of the Sanhedrin, during which they concoct an official charge to bring to the Romans (Mt 26:57-68). John will also omit this proceeding.

Jesus responds in verses 20-21 by confronting the hypocrisy of having been arrested so covertly. He has spoken openly all along, in synagogues and in the temple court. They should question the ones who heard him speak. He is making a point of law. For this Jesus is struck in the face by one of the guards, a flagrant violation of the law. Jesus' protest in verse 23 falls on deaf ears. He has allowed himself to be placed under the authority of a regime that is out of control in its abuse of power.

Jesus is bound and sent to Caiaphas.

PETER'S FINAL DENIALS

²⁵Now Simon Peter was standing and warming himself. They said to him, "You aren't one of His disciples too, are you?"

He denied it and said, "I am not!"

²⁶One of the high priest's slaves, a relative of the man whose ear Peter had cut off, said, "Didn't I see you with Him in the garden?"

²⁷Peter then denied it again. Immediately a rooster crowed.

*J*ohn presents the second and third denials of Peter in the scope of only three verses. He will, however, be the only evangelist to tell the story of Peter's restoration (Jn 21:15-19).

The second person who questions Peter asks the same question as the slave girl had, whether he is another of Jesus' disciples. Once again, it is important to realize that John is there with Peter as an acknowledged follower. Peter's response is not based on a simple fear of being exposed as some sort of spy. The reasons for his denial run much deeper. To the second question Peter gives the identical response.

Luke tells us the third question came an hour later (Lk 22:59). Peter has had time to brood over his situation. Matthew says the questioners noticed Peter's Galilean accent (Mt 26:73). John, with his local knowledge, adds the detail that this person was a relative of Malchus. The man observes that he saw Peter with Jesus in the olive grove. John does not give Peter's response. Matthew and Mark tell us Peter called down curses on himself at the third denial. Only Luke, who was not an eyewitness, gives the heartbreaking detail that at precisely this moment Peter's eyes met Jesus' across the courtyard. Jesus was "gazing" at Peter. Luke uses the same word (*emblepo*) used in John 1:42 to describe the way Jesus looked at Peter when he first called him.

Clearly the third question was the most focused and intense. To add to the intensity, Peter hears the rooster crow, the sign Jesus had given to him just after he had washed Peter's feet (Jn 13:38).

JESUS AND PILATE

28Then they took Jesus from Caiaphas to the governor's headquarters. It was early morning. They did not enter the headquarters themselves; otherwise they would be defiled and unable to eat the Passover.

29Then Pilate came out to them and said, "What charge do you bring against this man?"

30They answered him, "If this man weren't a criminal, we wouldn't have handed Him over to you."

31So Pilate told them, "Take Him yourselves and judge Him according to your law."

"It's not legal for us to put anyone to death," the Jews declared. 32They said this so that Jesus' words might be fulfilled signifying what kind of death He was going to die.

33Then Pilate went back into the headquarters, summoned Jesus, and said to Him, "Are You the King of the Jews?"

34Jesus answered, "Are you asking this on your own, or have others told you about Me?"

35"I'm not a Jew, am I?" Pilate replied. "Your own nation and the chief priests handed You over to me. What have You done?"

36"My kingdom is not of this world," said Jesus. "If My kingdom were of this world, My servants would fight, so that I wouldn't be handed over to the Jews. As it is, My kingdom does not have its origin here."

37"You are a king then?" Pilate asked.

"You say that I'm a king," Jesus replied. "I was born for this, and I have come into the world for this: to testify to the truth. Everyone who is of the truth listens to My voice."

38"What is truth?" said Pilate.

After he had said this, he went out to the Jews again and told them, "I find no grounds for charging Him. 39You have a custom that I release one prisoner to you at the Passover. So, do you want me to release to you the King of the Jews?"

40They shouted back, "Not this man, but Barabbas!" Now Barabbas was a revolutionary.

*A*fter the early morning hearing, which John omits, Jesus is taken to the governor's headquarters, in Latin the praetorium, or the home of the praetor. Jesus is brought early in the morning because this is the time of day when Roman officials would get their work done and receive their clients. From midday onward, influential Romans observed a day of organized leisure, primarily at the baths. The Jews knew they must get to Pilate early.

As Judean Jews, their Passover will be held this evening. Jesus and his disciples, Galilean Jews who observed the diaspora tradition of celebrating the meal on Thursday, have already observed their Passover. John does not introduce Pilate. He does not need to. Pilate was well-known to his first readers.

We know a lot about Pontius Pilate. He was in office A.D. 26–36. By this time he has already had a few major run-ins with the Jewish community, which he so detests. He has stolen money from the temple treasury to build an aqueduct. This caused a riot. He initially refused to remove the standards of his Roman soldiers, which bore forbidden images. This caused a riot in his capital in Caesarea. Eventually, he would be called back to Rome by Tiberius for atrocities against the Samaritans. While in route, Tiberius died and Pilate disappeared. It is believed he killed himself.

By far the most important piece of background in regard to Pilate is the fact that he received his position as a result of his friendship with Aelius Sejanus. Sejanus had been appointed Roman consul in A.D. 31 and secretly plotted to overthrow Tiberius. As consul, he was virtually a co-emperor. On October 18 of the same year the plot was uncovered and he was summarily executed. Tiberius ordered that Sejanus's anti-Jewish edicts were to be annulled, that "atrocities against the Jews would cease." This provides a window into Pilate's position now in A.D. 33. He is sitting on a powder keg in Jerusalem and will do anything to keep from igniting it, including handing over an innocent man to be crucified.

When Pilate routinely asks for the charges in verse 29, the Jews do not respond with any. They only insinuate that Jesus is a criminal. Pilate's first response is telling. He does not want to be involved in their religious disputes. He wants to get on with his day of organized leisure.

Verse 31 reveals the fact that Jesus' accusers intended to have him executed, and they want Pilate to do it for them. Here John reminds us that Jesus' words are being fulfilled for a second time. Faced with the dilemma, Pilate decides to interrogate Jesus. He has him brought into the Praetorium. Apparently there is no concern for Jesus' becoming unclean.

Their conversation reflects Pilate's ill humor and desire to be rid of Jesus. He impatiently snaps back at Jesus, "I'm not a Jew." Having initially asked Jesus if he thought himself a king in verse 33, Jesus responds in verse 36 that his kingdom is not of this world.

Pilate believes he has manipulated Jesus into a confession. "You are a king then?" he quips. Jesus responds affirmatively in verse 37. He was born to be a king, the kind of king who testifies to the truth.

So many sermons have been preached on Pilate's wistful question, "What is truth?" as if he was somehow drawn into the mystery of who Jesus might be. John's Gospel, however, gives no grounds for this interpretation of the story. Pilate does not linger to hear an answer from Jesus. He turns and abruptly leaves. His tone throughout is impatient and irritated. He goes out to the waiting Jews and reports there is no basis for a charge, much less a death sentence.

Critics of the New Testament like to point out that there is no reference in the ancient records of a Roman official routinely releasing a prisoner in honor of Passover. Roman law did provide that amnesty could be granted before sentence was passed. This may have been the basis for the observance. Pilate offers Jesus, who he refers to as "King of the Jews," a title he will repeatedly use to get under the skin of the Jewish officials.

The crowd refuses and asks instead for Barabbas, who had been convicted already of insurrection. The chief priests stirred up the rabble, telling them to shout for Barabbas instead (Mt 27:20; Mk 15:11).

JOHN 19

AMICUS CAESARIS

¹*Then Pilate took Jesus and had Him flogged.* ²*The soldiers also twisted together a crown of thorns, put it on His head, and threw a purple robe around Him.* ³*And they repeatedly came up to Him and said, "Hail, King of the Jews!" and were slapping His face.*

⁴*Pilate went outside again and said to them, "Look, I'm bringing Him outside to you to let you know I find no grounds for charging Him."*

⁵*Then Jesus came out wearing the crown of thorns and the purple robe. Pilate said to them, "Here is the man!"*

⁶*When the chief priests and the temple police saw Him, they shouted, "Crucify! Crucify!"*

Pilate responded, "Take Him and crucify Him yourselves, for I find no grounds for charging Him."

⁷*"We have a law," the Jews replied to him, "and according to that law He must die, because He made Himself the Son of God."*

⁸*When Pilate heard this statement, he was more afraid than ever.* ⁹*He went back into the headquarters and asked Jesus, "Where are You from?" But Jesus did not give him an answer.* ¹⁰*So Pilate said to Him, "You're not talking to me? Don't You know that I have the authority to release You and the authority to crucify You?"*

¹¹*"You would have no authority over Me at all," Jesus answered him, "if it hadn't been given you from above. This is why the one who handed Me over to you has the greater sin."*

¹²*From that moment Pilate made every effort to release Him. But the Jews shouted, "If you release this man, you are not Caesar's friend. Anyone who makes himself a king opposes Caesar!"*

¹³*When Pilate heard these words, he brought Jesus outside. He sat down on the judge's bench in a place called the Stone Pavement (but in Hebrew Gabbatha).* ¹⁴*It was the preparation day for the Passover, and it was about six in the morning. Then he told the Jews, "Here is your king!"*

¹⁵*But they shouted, "Take Him away! Take Him away! Crucify Him!"*

Pilate said to them, "Should I crucify your king?"

"We have no king but Caesar!" the chief priests answered.

¹⁶*So then, because of them, he handed Him over to be crucified. Therefore they took Jesus away.*

*T*he excruciating nature of the flogging of Jesus is often misunderstood. First, he did not receive thirty-nine stripes. That was the prescription for Jewish synagogue discipline that Paul boasted of having received five times (2 Cor 11:24). Jesus received a Roman flogging administered with a flagellum, a collection of heavy leather straps into which bone, glass and lead balls were embedded. There was no stipulation for how many lashes a person would receive, only that the person would be flogged until the flesh hung from his back. Prisoners were frequently disemboweled by flogging. Josephus tells us that he once witnessed a Roman flogging and reported that the internal organs of the victim became visible.[1] Usually a convicted criminal was flogged before crucifixion to hasten his death due to blood loss and shock. But Jesus' flogging is different. Pilate orders it before any sentence has been passed in order to appease the Jews (see Lk 23:15-16). Jesus is abused by the Roman soldiers, wrapped in a purple robe and crowned with thorns. If you look closely at the Gospels, it appears Pilate has done this hoping that the Jews will see the blood-soaked Jesus and be satisfied. In verse 4 he brings Jesus back out to the crowd and repeats that he finds Jesus innocent. The "here is the man" (v. 5) was spoken with a token of pity. He is not a king after all, but a frail, bleeding man. That Pilate would have a person he considered innocent flogged is a sign of how insane the whole proceedings were.

When the chief priests see Jesus bloodied, they are not satisfied. In fact, they become frenzied. They shout that they want him crucified. The examples of flagrant violation of Roman law keep piling up as Pilate commands the Jews to take Jesus and crucify him themselves, once more protesting his innocence. To hand an innocent man over to mob violence was the extreme opposite of the idea of the peace of Rome, the Pax Romana. In verse 7 the scene intensifies as the Jews bring a new charge, one that Pilate has not yet heard. Jesus claimed to be the Son of God. This involves the charge of blasphemy in Jewish law (Lev 24:14-16).

Pilate's response in verse 8 is fear. This is a serious charge in his Roman world. Only Caesar could lay claim to be the Son of God. Any claim against the sovereignty of Caesar by Jesus must be investigated. If word got back to Rome that Pilate had ignored this crime, he could lose his already precarious position.

He goes back into the Praetorium with a new question for Jesus. "Where are you from?" Perhaps he expects to hear the answer "heaven." This is a question that has swirled around Jesus since John 6:41 when he claimed to be the bread that came from heaven. Again, at the Feast of Tabernacles the crowd was confused about where Jesus was from (Jn 7:27-30, 41-43, 52).

By this point Jesus may be going into shock from the flogging. To be sure he has already lost a lot of blood. Perhaps he sees the discussion as pointless now and ignores Pilate's question. This infuriates Pilate, who tries to remind Jesus of his power of life and death over him, a power which Jesus says is only an illusion, as all earthly power is illusory. Pilate has no power except the power given to him from heaven, the place where Jesus is from. Then, remarkably, Jesus extends a measure of forgiveness, telling Pilate that the one who handed him over is more guilty than he. This expression of grace, something completely foreign to Pilate's world, has a seismic effect on the Roman governor. "From that moment" he decided that Jesus must be set free.

At precisely the same moment the Jews play their most powerful card. They capitalize on Pilate's insecurity in light of the Sejanus incident. They know exactly where his Achilles' heel is.

"If you release this man, you are not Caesar's friend."

If one simple moment in the trial of Jesus can be seen as pivotal, it is this moment. The "friends of Caesar" (amici Caesaris) were a well-defined group of senators, knights and powerful men of Rome who for one reason or another had merited the emperor's favor. Sejanus had been an amicis Caesaris before his plot was discovered. Pilate, as a Roman governor, would have been a member of this elite club as well. If he were to release someone who had claimed kingship, who considered himself a Son of God, Pilate would undoubtedly forfeit his membership in the friends of Caesar club. That was the deal breaker. Pilate would not hand Jesus over to the mob. He would pronounce the formal sentence of crucifixion, "you shall mount the cross" (*ibis in crucem*), himself. He would take the credit. He became their perfect pawn.

To make the proceedings now as official as possible, Pilate goes to the place where formal sentences are pronounced, the Stone Pavement. Julius Caesar carried a portable pavement with him on his campaigns for holding his tribunals. The Jews referred to the place as Gabbatha or "high place."

Verse 14 notes that it was preparation day, when Judean Jews were preparing to slaughter their Passover lambs, even as they are now preparing to sacrifice Jesus. It is noon, the sixth hour. Jesus' "hour" has finally come.

At this point Matthew tells us Pilate's wife sends word that he is to have nothing to do with this "righteous" man. She has been having nightmares about Jesus (Mt 27:19). But now it is too late.

Before, Pilate had pitifully exclaimed "Here is the man" (v. 5). Now he makes a pronouncement calculated to inflame the crowd who has used him and who he so despises. "Here is your king," he shouts. It has the desired effect. The crowd is whipped into a frenzy. Their repetitive statement "Take him away! Take him away!" reveals this. Then Pilate adds fuel to the flame. This is not the first time he has caused a riot. Is he supposed to crucify their king? he asks. Their response is another indication of the madness of any mob. Of all people, the chief priests cry out that Caesar is their only king. They want to be counted among the "friends of Caesar" as well.

EXCRUCIATING

[17] *Carrying His own cross, He went out to what is called Skull Place, which in Hebrew is called Golgotha.* [18] *There they crucified Him and two others with Him, one on either side, with Jesus in the middle.* [19] *Pilate also had a sign lettered and put on the cross. The inscription was:*

> *JESUS THE NAZARENE*
> *THE KING OF THE JEWS.*

[20] *Many of the Jews read this sign, because the place where Jesus was crucified was near the city, and it was written in Hebrew, Latin, and Greek.* [21] *So the chief priests of the Jews said to Pilate, "Don't write, 'The King of the Jews,' but that He said, 'I am the King of the Jews.'"*

²²*Pilate replied, "What I have written, I have written."*

²³*When the soldiers crucified Jesus, they took His clothes and divided them into four parts, a part for each soldier. They also took the tunic, which was seamless, woven in one piece from the top.* ²⁴*So they said to one another, "Let's not tear it, but cast lots for it, to see who gets it." They did this to fulfill the Scripture that says: They divided My clothes among themselves, and they cast lots for My clothing. And this is what the soldiers did.*

*T*he torture of the cross will forever be preserved for us in the word *excruciating*, which has at its root *crux* or *cross*. Since a flogging always preceded crucifixion, there is a chance that Jesus might have been whipped for a second time by the Roman soldiers.[2] He would have been led out with the other two criminals and taken to the place of crucifixion. The officials always chose the most public route to the place of crucifixion for maximum effect. The custom of forcing victims to carry their own cross beams is spoken of in ancient sources like Plutarch and Artemidorus. The location of Jesus' crucifixion is still debated. It was called the Place of the Skull. *Gulgolet* is the Hebrew word for skull, hence Golgotha. The Latin word for skull is calvaria, hence Calvary. Jesus is crucified between the other two criminals. No details are provided in any of the Gospels concerning Jesus' hands and feet being nailed to the cross. It is only after the resurrection that he shows them the wounds caused by the nails (Jn 20:20). John's description is typically sparse, "There they crucified him." His first readers did not need to hear the details of crucifixion. They had all witnessed multiple crucifixions in their lifetime. John is not interested in reporting the fulfillment of the Old Testament prophecy of Isaiah 53:12 that Jesus would be counted among the lawless (Mk 15:28).

Each one of the Gospels mentions the titulus, a notice that was fastened to Jesus' cross. John's version reads, "Jesus the Nazarene, the King of the Jews." Matthew gives us, "This is Jesus, the king of the Jews" (Mt 27:37). Mark's Gospel reads simply, "The king of the Jews" (Mk 15:26). Luke's version is "This is the king of the Jews" (Lk 23:38). What they all share in common is the title "King of the Jews." This was Pilate's sick joke on the Jews. In verse 21 they protest and ask Pilate to change the wording to read, "He said, 'I am the king of the Jews.'" But Pilate enigmatically responds that he has written what he has written, and there is nothing they can do about it.

From verse 23 we can deduce that four soldiers were assigned to the detachment that crucified Jesus, because his clothes were divided into four shares. Only John mentions the division of the clothes, referring specifically to the seamless tunic, which was a special prize. The soldiers, not wanting to tear it into four pieces, do what soldiers have done throughout the ages—cast dice to decide who would get it. John, who makes only one other reference to Old Testament fulfillment during the crucifixion, makes his first reference here. He quotes Psalm 22:18. Perhaps John is interested in this item because of his relationship with Mary, Jesus' mother. It was customary for mothers to make a seamless tunic to be presented as a gift to their sons when they left home. Mary will appear in the very next verse. Perhaps the detail was dear to John because the seamless tunic was dear to Mary.

THE WOMEN

²⁵Standing by the cross of Jesus were His mother, His mother's sister, Mary the wife of Clopas, and Mary Magdalene. ²⁶When Jesus saw His mother and the disciple He loved standing there, He said to His mother, "Woman, here is your son." ²⁷Then He said to the disciple, "Here is your mother." And from that hour the disciple took her into his home.

John lists four women who are hovering near the cross. The first is Jesus' mother, Mary. Next he refers to "Mary's sister." This is probably Salome (Mk 15:40). She is John's mother (Mt 27:56). Also there is Clopas's wife, also named Mary. We have no other reference to her in the New Testament. Finally there is Mary of Magdala. Her presence is also mentioned in both Matthew 27:56 and Mark 15:40. In Luke 8:2 we are told that she had been delivered of seven demons earlier in the ministry of Jesus. Luke will also make reference to her after the resurrection (Lk 24:10). In John's Gospel she will be a major character in the postresurrection ap-

pearances. In verse 26 Jesus looks down and sees his mother standing
next to the "disciple he loved." This is almost certainly the young John.
Even now, Jesus' thoughts center on her and her need for provision after
he is gone. He says to Mary that John is her son now, and to John that
Mary is his mother. John goes on to explain in verse 27 that he acted on
Jesus' words and took her home. Perhaps John needed Mary as much as
she needed him. Jesus' provision is not a slight on his brothers, as is
sometimes suggested. They are not there. John is, and he is a relative,
after all.

"IT IS FINISHED"

*28After this, when Jesus knew that everything was now accomplished that
the Scripture might be fulfilled, He said, "I'm thirsty!" 29A jar full of sour
wine was sitting there; so they fixed a sponge full of sour wine on hyssop and
held it up to His mouth.*

*30When Jesus had received the sour wine, He said, "It is finished!" Then
bowing His head, He gave up His spirit.*

*31Since it was the preparation day, the Jews did not want the bodies to
remain on the cross on the Sabbath (for that Sabbath was a special day). They
requested that Pilate have the men's legs broken and that their bodies be taken
away. 32So the soldiers came and broke the legs of the first man and of the
other one who had been crucified with Him. 33When they came to Jesus, they
did not break His legs since they saw that He was already dead. 34But one of
the soldiers pierced His side with a spear, and at once blood and water came
out. 35He who saw this has testified so that you also may believe. His testimony is true, and he knows he is telling the truth. 36For these things happened
so that the Scripture would be fulfilled: Not one of His bones will be broken.
37Also, another Scripture says: They will look at the One they pierced.*

John omits most of the details found in the Synoptics regarding the
crucifixion. He does not mention the three hours of darkness (Mt 27:45;
Mk 15:33; Lk 23:44). True to form he records a statement none of the
other Gospels give us, Jesus saying he was thirsty. John introduces this
part of the story hinting that Jesus deliberately spoke these words so

that the Scriptures would be fulfilled. Interestingly, John does not say which Scriptures (see Ps 22:15; 69:21). Both Matthew and Mark tell us the soldiers offered Jesus a drink. That the sponge is placed on a hyssop stalk indicates that Jesus was crucified on a high cross. He was offered wine that has spoiled and turned into vinegar. This was often given to soldiers when they were on duty. Jesus tastes the vinegar and pronounces "It is finished." John omits Luke's, "Into your hands I entrust my spirit" (Lk 23:46).

With these final words Jesus "gave up" his spirit. In John 10:18 he explained that he had received from the Father the ability to let go of his life and to take it up once more. Here he exercises that first "command." No one took Jesus' life from him. He let go of it voluntarily.

John reminds us again that it is the preparation day (see also v. 14). The next day was a special Sabbath, that is, a Sabbath during Passover. Even though the priests had recently claimed that they had no king but Caesar, even though they participated in mob violence to crucify an innocent man, they are still scrupulous about their observance of the Sabbath, an issue over which they had so many disagreements with Jesus. They do not want the naked bodies left on the crosses during their special Sabbath, so they asked Pilate to have them removed. They assume that Jesus is still alive, or else they would not have asked that the legs be broken. This was done to hasten the death of someone on the cross. Once the support of the legs was taken away, the full weight of the body would bear on the chest, and the victim would quickly and "mercifully" suffocate. As they had expected, the two criminals on either side of Jesus are still breathing. So the soldiers dutifully broke their legs by means of a heavy wooden mallet. When they examined Jesus, he was already dead after so short a period of time. The longest anyone is said to have remained alive on the cross was eight days. Jesus hung there only six hours.

To make certain Jesus is truly deceased, one of the soldiers takes his spear and thrusts it up through the body, under the ribs and into the heart. Out of the wound flows both blood and water. This will have significance to John later as he refers to it in 1 John 5:6-8.

All through the Gospel John has whispered to us, explaining details and the motivations of his characters. In verses 35-36 a different voice appears to be whispering. Could it be the voice of the soldier who was actually present? They are the words of a formal testimony: "he who saw this has testified" and "his testimony is true." Was the soldier a part of John's community in Ephesus? The testimony is further enhanced by the fact that it fulfilled two Old Testament prophecies. First, that none of Jesus' bones would be broken, a detail related to the preparation of the Passover lamb in Exodus 12:46 (compare Ps 34:20). In preparing the lamb it can be pulled apart at the joint, but none of the bones are supposed to be broken. The fact that Jesus' crucifixion fulfilled even this minute detail amazes John. The second fulfillment is based on a prophecy from Zechariah 12:10 that says the one who is pierced will be looked upon by those who pierced him. This would be an especially meaningful word of prophecy for the one who just testified to what he himself had done to the body of Jesus.

TWO BRAVE PHARISEES

38After this, Joseph of Arimathea, who was a disciple of Jesus—but secretly because of his fear of the Jews—asked Pilate that he might remove Jesus' body. Pilate gave him permission, so he came and took His body away. 39Nicodemus (who had previously come to Him at night) also came, bringing a mixture of about 75 pounds of myrrh and aloes. 40Then they took Jesus' body and wrapped it in linen cloths with the aromatic spices, according to the burial custom of the Jews. 41There was a garden in the place where He was crucified. A new tomb was in the garden; no one had yet been placed in it. 42They placed Jesus there because of the Jewish preparation and since the tomb was nearby.

*F*or all of the bad press the Pharisees receive in the New Testament, never forget that the only two men with the courage to claim the body of Jesus were two Pharisees: Joseph of Arimathea and Nicodemus.

Mark tells us Joseph of Arimathea went "boldly" to Pilate and asked for the body (Mk 15:43). John tells us he is one of those secret disciples of Jesus (see Jn 12:42). Apparently, so is Nicodemus, who we first met in John 3:1-12. Three years ago he had come in the night to talk to Jesus about the new birth. Again in John 7:50, Nicodemus stood up to the leadership, asking how they could condemn someone without speaking to the person first. That story hints at what a brave man Nicodemus was.

Now the two of them come to claim the body. Nicodemus provides a costly bed of spices on which to lay the body. According to Jewish burial customs, they wrap the body in strips of fine linen and place it in a new garden tomb that had never been used before. The fact that it was unused indicates that it is fit to be used by a king. (Like the donkey on which no one had ever ridden that Jesus entered Jerusalem on.) Only Matthew tells us it was Joseph's own tomb (Mt 27:59-60). For the third time we are reminded that it is preparation day, that is, Friday, the day before the special Sabbath.

Wrapping a body and laying it on a bed of spices was step one of the two-step process of Jewish burial. The body would be left in the tomb for a year while the flesh decomposed and fell away from the bones. Step two involved a member of the family coming and washing the bones, placing them in an ossuary. Jesus did not need step two. He barely needed step one!

The courageous act of claiming and burying the body of Jesus would have been considered a supreme act of *hesed*. This might be another clue that Nicodemus and Joseph were followers of Hillel, who is still regarded as the father of the Hasidic (those who do *hesed*) movement.

JOHN 20

NO EXPESTATIONS

¹On the first day of the week Mary Magdalene came to the tomb early, while it was still dark. She saw that the stone had been removed from the tomb. ²So she ran to Simon Peter and to the other disciple, the one Jesus loved, and said to them, "They have taken the Lord out of the tomb, and we don't know where they have put Him!"

³At that, Peter and the other disciple went out, heading for the tomb. ⁴The two were running together, but the other disciple outran Peter and got to the tomb first. ⁵Stooping down, he saw the linen cloths lying there, yet he did not go in. ⁶Then, following him, Simon Peter came also. He entered the tomb and saw the linen cloths lying there. ⁷The wrapping that had been on His head was not lying with the linen cloths but was folded up in a separate place by itself. ⁸The other disciple, who had reached the tomb first, then entered the tomb, saw, and believed. ⁹For they still did not understand the Scripture that He must rise from the dead. ¹⁰Then the disciples went home again.

*T*he Sabbath has been over only a few hours. Even though it is still dark, Mary of Magdala is on the way to the tomb of Jesus. In a world that comes to a grinding halt when the sun goes down, a small group of three women out in the dark morning is a sign of special dedication. Mark tells us the group included Mary of Magdala, Mary the mother of James (who we know nothing about) and Salome. John is only interested in Mary of Magdala's experience. In verse 3 she will tell Peter that "'we' don't know where they have put him," indicating the presence of the other women. The Synoptics tell us she had come with the women to anoint the body of Jesus. That is, to finish preparing the corpse because only hasty preparations were made after Jesus was placed in the tomb because of the Sabbath. Stop and realize what the implications are. The women are coming to anoint a corpse. They have absolutely no expectations that Jesus will rise from the dead, as he repeatedly said he would. When Mary sees that the heavy stone has been rolled away, she assumes that someone has come and moved the body. It is simply not in the realm of possibility for her, or any of the others, that Jesus has risen.

She runs to Peter, who is with the "other disciple," John. They become constant companions after the resurrection. In the book of Acts they are always together, like big brother and little brother. John never opens his mouth.

Peter and John respond to Mary's news by running to the tomb to see for themselves. John wants us to know specifically that he, being so much younger at the time, outran Peter. This is the kind of fact an elderly person like John would especially enjoy telling and retelling. The rest of the Gospel will be filled with small eyewitness details like this. John stops outside the tomb and looks inside, perhaps he wanted to avoid becoming unclean. When Peter arrives he observes none of the precautions and goes straight in (v. 6).

Verses 6-7 describe the contents of the tomb. It had not been ransacked by grave robbers. The strips of linen that had been wrapped around the body were literally "lying in their folds," as if the body had simply evaporated through them. The sweat cloth (*soudarion*) that had been wrapped around Jesus' face was folded up separately, indicating a lack of haste. In verse 8 John tells us he saw the conditions of the tomb and believed. He would be the first of Jesus' disciples to believe in the resurrected Lord. It's important to note that he believed without seeing Jesus himself. Luke tells us Peter left the tomb "wondering to himself what had happened" (Lk 24:12 NIV). John whispers the explanation in verse 9, that they had not yet put all of this together with the Scriptures.

ANGELIC QUESTIONS

¹¹But Mary stood outside facing the tomb, crying. As she was crying, she stooped to look into the tomb. ¹²She saw two angels in white sitting there, one at the head and one at the feet, where Jesus' body had been lying. ¹³They said to her, "Woman, why are you crying?"

"Because they've taken away my Lord," she told them, "and I don't know where they've put Him." ¹⁴Having said this, she turned around and saw Jesus standing there, though she did not know it was Jesus.

¹⁵"Woman," Jesus said to her, "why are you crying? Who is it you are looking for?"

Supposing He was the gardener, she replied, "Sir, if you've removed Him, tell me where you've put Him, and I will take Him away."

[16]Jesus said, "Mary."

Turning around, she said to Him in Hebrew, "Rabbouni!"—which means "Teacher."

[17]"Don't cling to Me," Jesus told her, "for I have not yet ascended to the Father. But go to My brothers and tell them that I am ascending to My Father and your Father—to My God and your God."

[18]Mary Magdalene went and announced to the disciples, "I have seen the Lord!" And she told them what He had said to her.

*U*ntil you engage with your imagination and understand that Mary is a person who, at this point, has literally lost everything, you cannot understand the next few verses. Peter and John leave while she lingers outside the tomb weeping. Having been traumatized by seeing Jesus brutally crucified, she now believes someone has stolen his body.

She looks down into the tomb and sees two angels sitting at the head and the foot of the slab where Jesus' body had been. Angelic questions usually indicate that the person being addressed has no idea of what is really going on (see, for example, Acts 1:11). Their question is no different. The angels inhabit a different reality. They know what has really occurred. To them it is a reasonable question. Why is she crying? What on earth is there to weep about?

Mary is sniffling out her answer when she senses someone behind her. Listen carefully to the text. She turns around before Jesus speaks. Jesus repeats the angels' question but adds, "Who is it you are looking for?"

This scene makes it clear that Mary had absolutely no expectations of seeing Jesus. That is why she assumes that this person is someone who takes care of the burial garden. How could it possibly be Jesus?

She responds to the "gardener" with the ridiculous prospect that if he will tell her where the body is she will go, by herself, and bring it back. Mary always leads with her heart. She had heard his voice already and had not recognized that it was Jesus. There was something about the way he said her name that made her aware of who he was. She calls out,

"Rabboni," literally the possessive form that means, "My teacher."

She falls at Jesus' feet and clings for dear life. She is not going to lose him again. His response in verse 17 is playful. It could be paraphrased "You don't have to cling to me; I haven't left yet!" Mary is privileged to be the first one to see Jesus, and now he entrusts to her what must have been the most completely satisfying words he had ever spoken. He was ascending, Jesus said, to his Father and to their Father, to his God and to their God. Because of all he had endured, Jesus made it possible for his Father to truly be our Father. The tone of his voice as he spoke those words is beyond any of our imaginations.

In verse 18 Mary obediently goes to the Eleven with the message. Luke tells us her words sounded like "nonsense" to the disciples (Lk 24:11).

A JOY NO ONE CAN TAKE

¹⁹*In the evening of that first day of the week, the disciples were gathered together with the doors locked because of their fear of the Jews. Then Jesus came, stood among them, and said to them, "Peace to you!"*

²⁰*Having said this, He showed them His hands and His side. So the disciples rejoiced when they saw the Lord.*

²¹*Jesus said to them again, "Peace to you! As the Father has sent Me, I also send you." ²²After saying this, He breathed on them and said, "Receive the Holy Spirit. ²³If you forgive the sins of any, they are forgiven them; if you retain the sins of any, they are retained."*

*T*hat evening, apparently after the Emmaus appearance in Luke 24, Jesus finally appears to the Eleven. They are locked away in fear, assuming that they might be next to be arrested. Jesus greets them with a very ordinary "*Shalom leka.*" He will repeat the greeting twice. Notice that he does not point to his familiar face but rather first shows them the scars in his hands and side. Jesus, the Lamb who was slain from the foundation of the world, is always recognized by his scars. In John 16:22 Jesus had promised them this moment, a time when they would experience the transforming joy that no one would ever be able to take away from them. This is that moment!

In verse 21 Jesus passes the key of his identity on to his disciples. Throughout the Gospel of John, Jesus has been the One who was sent, the Father was the One who had sent him. Now Jesus tells the Eleven he is sending them. They will be clothed with his authority. They will bear a concealed dignity. They are now the sent ones.

In a symbolic gesture he breathes on them saying, "Receive the Holy Spirit." He had spoken so much about the Spirit during their last hours together (Jn 16:5-15). Now he imparts the Spirit by his breath (see Gen 2:7; Ezek 37:5).

Their principal assignment? To forgive sin. Jesus' death and resurrection has made such forgiveness possible. Now his sent ones must proclaim and offer that forgiveness. He closes with a warning. If they do not forgive, if they refuse to display his forgiveness in their lives, people will not find forgiveness, and it will not be displayed at all.

"I WILL NEVER BELIEVE!"

24 But one of the Twelve, Thomas (called "Twin"), was not with them when Jesus came. 25 So the other disciples kept telling him, "We have seen the Lord!"

But he said to them, "If I don't see the mark of the nails in His hands, put my finger into the mark of the nails, and put my hand into His side, I will never believe!"

26 After eight days His disciples were indoors again, and Thomas was with them. Even though the doors were locked, Jesus came and stood among them. He said, "Peace to you!"

27 Then He said to Thomas, "Put your finger here and observe My hands. Reach out your hand and put it into My side. Don't be an unbeliever, but a believer."

28 Thomas responded to Him, "My Lord and my God!"

29 Jesus said, "Because you have seen Me, you have believed. Those who believe without seeing are blessed."

We first met Thomas in John 11:16 with his dismal, loyal despair saying that they should go and die with Jesus. John does not tell us why, but

Thomas was not present for the first joyful reunion. When he heard about it, he was incredulous. I believe Thomas's doubt should be applauded more often. Kierkegaard said, "Only he who doubts can truly believe." It is important to note that Thomas is never condemned by Jesus for doubting. Thomas declares in verse 25 that unless he sees the proof of the wounds, he will not believe.

Thomas was forced to wait an entire week. It is difficult to imagine what must have gone through his mind during those days as he heard the others give their accounts of seeing the risen Jesus.

Once again they are locked away, still looking over their shoulders, afraid that another armed cohort might come and find them. Again Jesus appears through the locked doors with the ever ordinary "Peace to you." It would be like one of us simply saying "Hi."

Jesus' words to Thomas are almost playful. Literally, he says in verse 27, "Bring your finger over here!" There is no word of Thomas actually examining the wounds. All we can be certain of is his breathless response, "My Lord and my God."

The tension between seeing and believing must be maintained, as the preference for believing without seeing must also be maintained (1 Pet 1:8). Jesus observes that they have finally come to believe because they have seen him. Then, remarkably, he pronounces a blessing, a *berakah*, on those of us who have come to believe in him without seeing. In John 17:20 Jesus revealed that we were already on his mind and in his prayers. Here, as the disciples gather around, once again he thinks of us and pronounces his blessing!

THE FIRST CONCLUSION

30Jesus performed many other signs in the presence of His disciples that are not written in this book. 31But these are written so that you may believe Jesus is the Messiah, the Son of God, and by believing you may have life in His name.

These two brief verses represent the original ending of John's Gospel. Verse 30 is one of the most frustrating verses in the Bible. There were any number of other signs Jesus performed, but they are not recorded in this book. (John, how could you do this to those of us who hunger for more detail?) Verse 31 contains the purpose of the book—why John wrote it and what he deeply hopes will happen in the hearts of everyone who reads it. It has not been a biography. None of the Gospels are biographies. If they were then more of the scenes mentioned in verse 30 would be woven into these pages. The Gospels are testimonies. They are perfect testimonies. The Gospel of John was written so that we might believe and in believing have life in his name.

JOHN 21

THE PERSISTENCE OF DOUBT

¹After this, Jesus revealed Himself again to His disciples by the Sea of Tiberias. He revealed Himself in this way:

²Simon Peter, Thomas (called "Twin"), Nathanael from Cana of Galilee, Zebedee's sons, and two others of His disciples were together.

³"I'm going fishing," Simon Peter said to them.

"We're coming with you," they told him. They went out and got into the boat, but that night they caught nothing.

⁴When daybreak came, Jesus stood on the shore. However, the disciples did not know it was Jesus.

⁵"Men," Jesus called to them, "you don't have any fish, do you?"

"No," they answered.

⁶"Cast the net on the right side of the boat," He told them, "and you'll find some." So they did, and they were unable to haul it in because of the large number of fish. ⁷Therefore the disciple, the one Jesus loved, said to Peter, "It is the Lord!"

When Simon Peter heard that it was the Lord, he tied his outer garment around him (for he was stripped) and plunged into the sea. ⁸But since they were not far from land (about 100 yards away), the other disciples came in the boat, dragging the net full of fish. ⁹When they got out on land, they saw a charcoal fire there, with fish lying on it, and bread.

¹⁰"Bring some of the fish you've just caught," Jesus told them. ¹¹So Simon Peter got up and hauled the net ashore, full of large fish—153 of them. Even though there were so many, the net was not torn.

¹²"Come and have breakfast," Jesus told them. None of the disciples dared ask Him, "Who are You?" because they knew it was the Lord. ¹³Jesus came, took the bread, and gave it to them. He did the same with the fish.

¹⁴This was now the third time Jesus appeared to the disciples after He was raised from the dead.

I n chapter 21 we have two unique postresurrection accounts: the second miraculous catch of fish and an extended discussion with Peter beside the lake. It is widely accepted that chapter 21 was appended to the Gospel after John's death. Chapter 20 ended with a literary conclusion. The language shifts in chapter 21. There are phrases and new vocabulary that appear nowhere else in the Gospel, indicating a different author. In the latter part of the chapter there is an explanation for a confused rumor involving John's death (v. 23). Many see this as the reason for chapter 21. John, who had lived to be one hundred years old, has finally died, and the false rumor concerning his death needs to be explained.

Matthew tells us that after the resurrection Jesus met with his disciples back in Galilee. Luke 5 presents the story of the first miraculous catch of fish, early in the ministry of Jesus. Peter was also the focus of that story. At that time he fell at Jesus' feet and begged for something he really did not want, for Jesus to go away. Now Jesus has returned from the grave. This is the second miraculous catch. As the miracle is repeated, Peter will be confronted by Jesus and will receive encouragement once again.

The story takes place by the Sea of Galilee, which is always referred to as "Tiberius" in John's Gospel (Jn 6:1). The phrase at the close of verse 1, "it happened this way" (NIV), occurs nowhere else in the Gospel. Seven of the Eleven are fishing once more at Peter's invitation. They are home once again, where Jesus has told them to wait for him. Perhaps this was a way to create some much-needed income. Similar to the first miraculous catch, they are completely unsuccessful after a night's fishing.

At dawn they see someone standing on the shore. They are roughly one hundred yards from the beach and do not recognize Jesus. It is interesting to note that no one immediately recognizes Jesus after the resurrection. Mary thought he was the gardener. Likewise, the disciples on the road to Emmaus do not recognize him (Lk 24:13-33). Jesus refers to the disciples as literally "children" (*paidion*). Nowhere else in the Gospel does he refer to them by this term. (In 13:33 he used a different term for children, *teknia*.) They haven't caught any fish, have they? Grammatically, Jesus' question expects the answer no.

The account is filled with eyewitness detail. John is certainly the source of the story, though he might not have actually written chapter 21. He remembers that Jesus told them to throw their nets over the right side of the boat. All at once the nets are overflowing with fish.

Finally, Jesus is recognized by John, but not because of his familiar face. Look closely at the text. John recognizes Jesus when he sees the net full of fish and must have remembered their earlier fishing experience, which is recorded in Luke 5. John realizes that there is only one person who can do this—Jesus!

Upon hearing John, Peter wraps his outer robe around him and dives into the lake. There is significant meaning in this. It reveals how deeply Peter wants to get back to Jesus. Their encounter on the shore is not the shaming it is frequently presented as being. Clearly, there is no shame left in Peter from the three denials. Jesus had appeared already to Peter in Jerusalem in an unrecorded postresurrection appearance (see Lk 24:34; 1 Cor 15:5). The denials had been dealt with then. There is no hesitation on Peter's part. He is anxious to be with his friend again, even if it means swimming one hundred yards in the cold lake.

When the other disciples land the boat, still towing the net full of fish (which was too large to haul into the boat), the disciples see a fire burning on the beach. It has already burned down to the coals (v. 9), another eyewitness detail. This indicates that Jesus may have been waiting for them for some time. There are fish and bread waiting, cooking on the coals. Jesus has prepared breakfast for them. The fact that no one comments on the breakfast (you might assume they would have protested, as Peter had done at the foot washing) says to me that this was nothing out of the ordinary. Perhaps Jesus always made breakfast for them. It would have been consistent with his character as servant Lord.

Peter single-handedly climbs up into the boat and drags the net to shore. The number of the fish, 153, is often seen as a cryptic symbol, as a puzzle that needs to be solved. I prefer to see it as yet another eyewitness detail. Fishermen are always proud of the number of fish they have caught, even when someone else helps them make the catch.

Verse 12 contains a mystery. As the disciples stand around the fire, looking at Jesus, none of them dared ask, "Who are you?" They knew it was the Lord, but something was still not immediately apparent. The persistence of doubt after the resurrection is a common theme in the Gospels. In Matthew 28:17, as the disciples gather around Jesus on a mountaintop in Galilee, he records that some of them still doubted.

PURE ENCOURAGEMENT

15When they had eaten breakfast, Jesus asked Simon Peter, "Simon, son of John, do you love Me more than these?"

"Yes, Lord," he said to Him, "You know that I love You."

"Feed My lambs," He told him.

16A second time He asked him, "Simon, son of John, do you love Me?"

"Yes, Lord," he said to Him, "You know that I love You."

"Shepherd My sheep," He told him.

17He asked him the third time, "Simon, son of John, do you love Me?"

Peter was grieved that He asked him the third time, "Do you love Me?" He said, "Lord, You know everything! You know that I love You."

"Feed My sheep," Jesus said. 18"I assure you: When you were young, you would tie your belt and walk wherever you wanted. But when you grow old, you will stretch out your hands and someone else will tie you and carry you where you don't want to go." 19He said this to signify by what kind of death he would glorify God. After saying this, He told him, "Follow Me!"

20So Peter turned around and saw the disciple Jesus loved following them. That disciple was the one who had leaned back against Jesus at the supper and asked, "Lord, who is the one that's going to betray You?" 21When Peter saw him, he said to Jesus, "Lord—what about him?"

22"If I want him to remain until I come," Jesus answered, "what is that to you? As for you, follow Me."

23So this report spread to the brothers that this disciple would not die. Yet Jesus did not tell him that he would not die, but, "If I want him to remain until I come, what is that to you?"

After the meal the spotlight is focused solely on Jesus and Peter. This passage is often referred to as the "reinstatement of Peter." The popular idea is that having denied Jesus three times, Peter is now given an opportunity to reaffirm his commitment three times, thus undoing his denials.

If we take seriously the unrecorded appearance to Peter in Jerusalem, surely more is going on here. The betrayal has been conclusively dealt with. Why else would Peter impetuously swim to Jesus? I prefer to see this as a story of Jesus providing pure encouragement to his friend who was so badly in need of it. Though he was forgiven, Peter might still be tempted to believe that he has forfeited his right to give leadership to the community. Jesus wants to encourage Peter that his acceptability is based on his love. There is nothing in his past that can disqualify him.

In verse 15 Jesus asks if Peter loves him more than "these." You must decide for yourself what *these* refers to. Is it the boats and the nets to which Peter has returned? Or is it the other disciples? Has Peter, in his newly restored confidence, boasted once more that he loves Jesus more than any of the others (see Mt 26:33; Mk 14:29, 31)?

The focus of their exchange should not be the varying uses of *agape* or *phileo*, but rather Jesus' threefold charge to Peter to feed his lambs, take care of his sheep, and feed his sheep.

Jesus is done speaking encouragement to his friend. Next he wants to arm Peter with the knowledge of his own death. He tells them that he will "stretch out his arms." The two most common metaphors for crucifixion were to be "lifted up" or to be "stretched out." Verse 19 makes it clear. Jesus was indicating how Peter would glorify God by his death on a cross. Remember by the time the Gospel is written, Peter has been dead for over twenty years.

The "follow me" of verse 19 is not the call to discipleship but the simple invitation to take a walk with Jesus along the shore. As they move down the beach, Peter looks back at the young John, who like a puppy is following the two men who have been like big brothers to him for the past three years. A parenthetical statement, much like John's other whisperings, explains, from the story of the Last Supper, who the disciple is. Peter asks a reasonable question, having just heard a prophetic word about how his life will end. "What about him?"

In his response Jesus is trying to focus Peter. But his statement was misunderstood. This is the last example of the motif of misunderstanding in the Gospel. The last words of Jesus are misunderstood! Jesus says that if he wants John to remain alive until he returns, what is that to Peter? Peter must follow him. (This is the big "follow me" of discipleship.)

Verse 23 explains the whole misunderstanding. Jesus never said John would not die. He was making a point to Peter. But, because of the misunderstanding, a rumor began that John would not die until Jesus returned. The most reasonable explanation for this passage is that indeed the hundred-year-old John has passed away. It is time for the rumor to be definitively dealt with. The voice of the different author of chapter 21 is detected in the "we" of verse 24.

THE FINAL CONCLUSION

²⁴*This is the disciple who testifies to these things and who wrote them down. We know that his testimony is true.*

²⁵*And there are also many other things that Jesus did, which, if they were written one by one, I suppose not even the world itself could contain the books that would be written.*

*T*he second conclusion, which echoes the first from John 20:30-31, brings the Gospel to its appropriate close. Again we hear those frustrating words that Jesus did many other things that were not recorded. To add to the frustration we are told that the whole world could not contain the books that might have been written about Jesus. In the centuries that followed, the books that spoke about Jesus have flowed by the thousands, and yet still the world is not full of them. In many, perhaps most, of those books Jesus remains the misunderstood Messiah. Misunderstood, not because he had been obtuse or obscure, but because the wisdom he spoke and embodied was not, could not be grasped only through the intellect. The wisdom Jesus was could only be comprehended through relationship with the Word who had become flesh.

APPENDIX A

Material Unique to John

1–3—Early Judean ministry

1:29-34—Jesus, the Lamb of God

1:43-51—Jesus with Nathanael

2:1-11—The wedding at Cana

2:12-25—First expulsion of the merchants from the temple

3:1-21—Jesus with Nicodemus

3:22-36—Disciples of Jesus baptizing in Judea

4:1-42—The woman at the well

4:43-54—Healing of the official's son in Cana of Galilee

5:1-15—Healing of the lame man by the pool of Bethesda

5:31-47—Testimonies about Jesus

6:8-9—Boy with the lunch

6:25-59—Jesus, the bread of life

6:60-71—Many disciples desert Jesus

7—Jesus at the Feast of Tabernacles

7:1-5—Unbelief of Jesus' brothers

7:53–8:11—Woman caught in adultery

9—Healing of the man born blind

11:1-44—Raising of Lazarus

12:20-28—Coming of the Greeks

12:27-33—The voice from heaven

13:1-17—Washing the disciples' feet

13:18–17:27—Jesus' final words to the Twelve

18:12-24—Jesus taken to Annas

19:38-42—Joseph of Arimathea receives permission to bury Jesus' body

20:10-18—Appearance to Mary Magdalene

20:24-29—Appearance to Thomas
21:1-14—Second miraculous catch
21:15-23—The final encouragement of Peter

APPENDIX B

The Motif of Misunderstanding

2:20—Jesus' statement about the "temple"

3:4, 9—Nicodemus misunderstands the new birth

4:15— The woman at the well misunderstands about the water

6:34— The people misunderstand concerning the bread

6:42—How can he say he came down from heaven?

6:52—How can he give us his flesh?

7:20—Who is trying to kill you?

7:27—No one will know where the Christ is from

7:35-36—Where will Jesus go?

8:22—Will he kill himself?

8:27—Misunderstanding about the Father

8:33—How can you say we will be set free?

8:57—You have seen Abraham?

10:6—The disciples misunderstand the image of the shepherd

11:12—The disciples misunderstand Lazarus's "sleep"

11:24—Martha misunderstands "your brother will rise"

12:34—Crowd misunderstands Jesus reference to "lifted up"

13:7—Peter doesn't understand the foot washing

14:5—Thomas misunderstands where Jesus is going

16:17-18—Disciples misunderstand "a little while"

21:22-23—Jesus' statement about John misunderstood

APPENDIX C

Occurrences of John's "Whispering"

1:28—"All this happened in Bethany"

1:39—"It was about 10 in the morning"

2:11—"Jesus performed this first sign"

2:21—"He was speaking about the sanctuary of His body"

2:24—"Jesus . . . would not entrust himself to them"

3:24—"John had not yet been thrown into prision"

4:8—"His disciples had gone into town to buy food"

4:9—"Jews do not associate with Samaritans"

4:45—"the Galilleans welcomed Him"

6:6—"He asked this to test him [Philip]"

6:59—"He said these things while teaching in the synagogue"

6:64—"For Jesus knew from the beginning . . . who would not believe"

6:71—"He was referring to Judas"

7:5—"not even His brothers believed in Him"

7:22—"not that it comes from Moses"

7:39—"He said this about the Spirit"

8:20—"He spoke these words by the treasury"

9:22-23—"His parents said these things because they were afraid"

11:13—"Jesus, however, was speaking about His death"

12:16—"His disciples did not understand these things"

18:10—"The slave's name was Malchus"

19:35—"He who saw this has testified" (Someone else whispering?)

20:9—"For they still did not understand the Scripture"

21:20—"That disciple was the one who had leaned back against Jesus"

APPENDIX D

The Prophet Like Moses

1:21—"Are you the Prophet?"

1:25—"Why then do you baptize if you aren't . . . the Prophet?"

1:45—"the One Moses wrote about in the Law"

3:34—"God sent Him, and He speaks God's words"

5:30—"I do not seek My own will, but the will of Him who sent Me"

7:16—"My teaching isn't Mine but is from the One who sent Me"

8:16—"I and the Father who sent Me judge together"

8:26—"what I have heard from Him—these things I tell the world"

8:38—"I speak what I have seen in the presence of the Father"

8:42—"I didn't come on My own, but He sent Me"

12:49—"I have not spoken on My own, but the Father Himself who sent Me" (Jesus' last public words)

14:10—"The words I speak to you I do not speak on My own"

15:15—"I have made known to you everything I have heard from My Father"

17:7—"Now they know that all things You have given to Me are from You"

NOTES

Preface

[1]Following the resurrection and the Pentecostal mention in Acts, tradition asserts that Mary lived either in Ephesus or in Jerusalem and that she may have been buried in Ephesus (Eusebius, *Historia Ecclesiastica* 3.31; 5.24, in *Patrologiae Graeca*, ed. Jacques-Paul Migne (Paris: Apud Garnier Fratres et J.-P. Migne Successores, 1864), 20:280, 493.
[2]See Craig S. Keener, *The Gospel of John: A Commentary* (Peabody, MA: Hendrickson, 2003), pp. 102-3, for a discussion of the implications of John's great age and a listing of other ancients who lived into their eighties and nineties.
[3]Irenaeus, *Against Heresies* 2.33, 3.3, quoted in Eusebius, *Church Histories* 3.23, ed. Paul Maier (Grand Rapids: Kregel, 1999), p. 110.
[4]Paul Trebilco, *The Early Christians in Ephesus from Paul to Ignatius* (Grand Rapids: Eerdmans, 2004), p. 11.
[5]Sjef van Tilborg, *Reading John in Ephesus* (New York: E. J. Brill, 1996), p. 147.
[6]Josephus, *Antiquities of the Jews* 14.223-27.
[7]Ibid., 16.167-8, 172-3.
[8]Ibid., 16.27-30, 163, 167-68, 172-73.
[9]For echoes of community conflict in John's Gospel see John 9:22; 12:42; 16:2.
[10]Tilborg, *Reading John in Ephesus*, p. 63.

John 1

[1]Many scholars agree that the Hebrew term *shaliah* is behind the Greek word for apostle (*apostolos*). Interestingly, though John focuses on Jesus as the "sent one" or authoritative representative, he never uses the word *apostle*.
[2]Babylonian Talmud *Ketubot* 96a.
[3]*Midraš Qohelet* 5.11.2.

John 2

[1]The name Bazaar of Annas is found in the Talmud (*Siphre* on Deut 10:5). Josephus mentions the greed of the high priest's family in *Antiquities of the Jews* 20.9.2-4.
[2]Mishnah *Bekorot* 8.7.
[3]Babylonian Talmud *Baba Batra* 4a.

John 3

[1]The Mishnah suggests the Sanherdin was composed of two courts, the Great Sanhedrin and the Lesser Sanhedrin (*m. Sanhedrin* 1.16). As best we can determine, in Jesus'

day the Sanhedrin was presided over by the high priest. It is roughly equivalent to our Supreme Court (Mt 26:59; Mk 15:1; Jn 11:47; Acts 5:27).

[2]In Jesus' day the Pharisees were in the process of dividing into two schools. The first and originally the most powerful were the Shammaites or followers of Shammai. They were known for their severity and separateness. They were anti-Gentile and argued that it would have been better if humans had never been created. The second school, though less popular in Jesus' day, would eventually win the hearts of the people, especially after a voice from heaven was heard to endorse them over the Shammaites. They were the Hillelites, the founders of the Jewish religion we know today. Their founder, Hillel, was famous for his gentleness and openness, especially to the Gentiles. He became known for his works of kindness (*hesed*). He was the spiritual father of the Hasidic movement. The Pharisees who oppose Jesus in the Gospels appear to be Shammaites. Nicodemus was almost certainly a follower of Hillel.

[3]See Justin Martyr, *First Apology* 54.10.

[4]Eusebius, *Church Histories* 3:24, ed. Paul Maier (Grand Rapids: Kregel, 1999), p. 114.

John 4

[1]Josephus, *Antiquities of the Jews* 20.1.8; *Life of Flavius Josephus* 269.

[2]Rabbi Eliezer, cited in *m. Shebiit* 8:10.

[3]When the Assyrians invaded the northern kingdom in 720 B.C., they resettled the land with foreigners who intermarried with the Jews who had been left behind. During the exile the importance of refraining from intermarrying took on enormous importance. Refusal to intermarry meant that Israel would survive as a nation. When the exiles returned, they looked upon those who had intermarried as squatters. They became the Samaritans (see Ezek 4; 2 Kings 17:6-24).

[4]Mishnah *Abot* 1.5.

John 5

[1]Mishnah *Shabbat* 7.2.

[2]Mishnah *Ketubot* 2.9.

John 6

[1]Babylonian Talmud *Berakot* 50b, 52b.

[2]Compare Matthew 15:29 and Mark 7:31 for the feeding of the four thousand. See also Matthew 16:9-10 for Jesus' description of the two feedings and use of the two separate terms for basket in his explanation.

[3]Verse 23 contains the only reference to the city of Tiberius in all of the Gospels. It was looked on as a pagan city owing to the fact that Herod the Great built the city over a graveyard.

John 7

[1]*Abot* 2.6.

John 8

[1]Josephus, *Antiquities of the Jews* 18.1.6. See Lev 25:39-42; Rom 6:17-18.

John 9

[1]Suetonius, *Lives of the Caesars* 10.7.

John 11

[1]Mishnah *Sanhedrin* 10.1.
[2]Josephus, *Jewish Wars* 2.8.14.

John 13

[1]Craig S. Keener, *IVP Background Commentary: New Testament* (Downers Grove, IL: IVP Academic, 1994), p. 308.

John 18

[1]Josephus, *Jewish Wars* 1.13.9.
[2]Geza Vermes, *Who's Who in the Age of Jesus* (New York: Penguin Reference Library, 2005), p. 44.

John 19

[1]William Whiston, ed., *Josephus: The Complete Works* (Grand Rapids: Kregel, 1960), p. 500.
[2]Clint E. Arnold, ed., *Zondervan Illustrated Bible Backgrounds Commentary* (Grand Rapids: Zondervan, 2002), 1:147.

RESOURCES

COMMENTARIES

Boring, M. Eugene, Klaus Berger, and Colpe Carsten. *Hellenistic Commentary to the New Testament*. Nashville: Abingdon Press, 1995.

Brown, Raymond E. *The Gospel and Epistles of John: A Concise Commentary*. Collegeville, MN: Liturgical Press, 1988.

Bruner, Frederick Dale. *The Gospel of John*. Grand Rapids: Eerdmans, 2012.

Keener, Craig S. *The Gospel of John: A Commentary*. Peabody, MA: Hendrickson, 2003.

———. *The Historical Jesus of the Gospels*. Grand Rapids: Eerdmanns, 2009.

———. *The IVP Bible Background Commentary: New Testament*. Downers Grove, IL: InterVarsity Press, 1993.

Lightfoot, John. *Commentary on the New Testament from the Talmud and Hebraica*. Vol. 3. Peabody, MA: Hendrickson, 1995.

Metzger, Louis Paul. *The Gospel of John: When Love Came to Town*. Downers Grove, IL: IVP Books, 2010.

Nyland, A. *John's Gospel: The Source New Testament*. Australia: Smith & Stirling, 2010.

Vanier, Jean. *Drawn into the Mystery of Jesus Through the Gospel of John*. Mahwah, NJ: Paulist Press, 2004.

LIFE SITUATIONS AND BACKGROUND STUDIES

Arnold, Clint E. *Zondervan Illustrated Bible Backgrounds Commentary*. Vol. 1. Grand Rapids: Zondervan, 2002.

Barnett, Paul. *The Birth of Christianity: The First Twenty Years*. Grand Rapids: Eerdmans, 2005.

Barrett, C. K. *The New Testament Background: Selected Documents*. San Francisco: Harper & Row, 1987.

Bauckham, Richard. *Jesus and the Eyewitnesses: The Gospels as Eyewitness Testimony*. Grand Rapids: Eerdmans, 2006.

Bell, Albert A. *Exploring the New Testament World.* Nashville: Thomas Nelson, 1998.

Brann, Eva. *The Logos of Heraclitus.* Philadelphia: Paul Dry, 2011.

Charlesworth, James H., and Loren L. Johns. *Hillel and Jesus: Comparative Studies of Two Major Religious Leaders.* Minneapolis: Fortress Press, 1997.

Cohick, Lynn H. *Women in the World of the Earliest Christians: Illuminating Ancient Ways of Life.* Grand Rapids: Baker Academic, 2009.

Connolly, Peter. *Living in the Time of Jesus of Nazareth.* Oxford: Oxford University Press, 1983.

Evans, Craig A. *Jesus and His World: The Archaeological Evidence.* Louisville: Westminster John Knox Press, 2012.

Ferguson, Everett. *Early Christians Speak: Faith and Life in the First Three Centuries.* Abilene, TX: Abilene Christian University Press, 1981.

Fitzmeyer, Joseph A. *The Semitic Background of the New Testament.* Grand Rapids: Eerdmans, 1997.

Fragments: The Collected Wisdom of Heraclitus. Translated by Brooks Haxton. New York: Penguin Putnam, 2001.

Gianotti, Charles R. *The New Testament and the Misnah; A Cross-Reference Index.* Grand Rapids: Baker, 1983.

Gower, Ralph. *The New Manners and Customs of Bible Times.* Chicago: Moody Press, 1987.

Grant, Michael. *A Guide to the Ancient World: A Dictionary of Classical Place Names.* New York: Barnes & Noble, 1986.

———. *Jesus.* New York: Charles Scribner's, 1977.

Green, Joel, and Scot McKnight, eds. *Dictionary of Jesus and the Gospels.* Downers Grove, IL: InterVarsity Press, 1992.

Harris, R. Laird, Gleason L. Archer, and Bruce K. Waltke. *Theological Wordbook of the Old Testament.* Chicago: Moody Press, 1980.

Instone-Brewer, David. *Traditions of the Rabbis from the Era of the New Testament.* Vols. 1-2. Grand Rapids: Eerdmans, 2004.

Keener, Craig S. *The Historical Jesus of the Gospels.* Grand Rapids: Eerdmans, 2009.

Lawrence, Paul. *The IVP Atlas of the Bible.* Downers Grove, IL: IVP Academic, 2006.

Leon-Dufour, Xavier. *Dictionary of the New Testament.* San Francisco: Harper & Row, 1980.

Lohse, Eduard. *The New Testament Environment.* Nashville: Abingdon Press, 1976.

Magness, Jodi. *Stone and Dung, Oil and Spit: Jewish Daily Life in the Time of Jesus.* Grand Rapids: Eerdmans, 2011.

Maier, Paul L. *Eusebius: The Church History.* Grand Rapids: Kregel, 1999.

Matthews, Victor H. *Manners and Customs in the Bible.* Peabody, MA: Hendrickson, 1991.

McReynolds, Paul R. *Word Study Greek-English New Testament.* Wheaton, IL: Tyndale House, 1966.

Meeks, Wayne A. *The First Urban Christians.* New Haven, CT: Yale University Press, 1983.

The Mishnah. Translated by Herbert Danby. Oxford: Oxford University Press, 1993.

Pliny the Younger: Complete Letters. Translated by P. G. Walsh. Oxford: Oxford University Press, 2006.

Reynolds, John Mark. *When Athens Met Jerusalem: An Introduction to Classical and Christian Thought.* Downers Grove, IL: IVP Academic, 2009.

Richardson, Peter. *Herod: King of the Jews and Friend of the Romans.* Minneapolis: Fortress Press, 1999.

Saldarini, Anthony J. *Pharisees, Scribes and Sadducees in Palestinian Society.* Grand Rapids: Eerdmans, 1988.

Schurer, Emil. *The Jewish People in the Time of Jesus.* New York: Schocken, 1978.

Scott, J. Julius. *Jewish Backgrounds of the New Testament.* Grand Rapids: Baker, 1995.

Skarsaune, Oskar. *In the Shadow of the Temple: Jewish Influences on Early Christianity.* Downers Grove, IL: InterVarsity Press, 2002.

Skarsaune, Oskar, and Reidar Hvalvik. *Jewish Believers in Jesus.* Peabody, MA: Hendrickson, 2007.

Strauss, Mark L. *Four Portraits, One Jesus.* Grand Rapids: Zondervan, 2007.

Throckmorton, Burton H. *Gospel Parallels.* Nashville: Thomas Nelson, 1967.

Tilborg, Sjef van. *Reading John in Ephesus.* New York: E. J. Brill, 1996.

Treblico, Paul. *The Early Christians in Ephesus from Paul to Ignatius.* Grand Rapids: Eerdmans, 2004.

Vermes, Geza. *Who's Who in the Age of Jesus.* New York: Penguin Reference Library, 2005.

Whiston, William. *Josephus: The Complete Works.* Grand Rapids: Kregel, 1960.

Wilken, Robert L. *The Christians as the Romans Saw Them.* New Haven, CT: Yale, 1984.

Zuzic, Marko. *A Short History of St. John of Ephesus.* Lima, OH: American Society of Ephesus, 1960.

ARTICLES

Balfour, Glenn. "The Jewishness of John's Use of the Scriptures in John 6:31 and 7:37-38." *Tyndale Bulletin* 46, no 2 (1995).

Baugh, S. M. "Cult Prostitution in New Testament Ephesus." *Journal of the Evangelical Theological Society* 42, no. 3 (September 1999).

Bird, Michael F. "The Formation of the Gospels in the Setting of Early Christianity: The Jesus Tradition As Corporate Memory." *Westminster Theological Journal* 67, no. 1 (spring 2005).

Carson, Donald A. "Understanding Misunderstandings in the Fourth Gospel." *Tyndale Bulletin* 33, no. 1 (1982).

Dvorak, James D. "The Relationship Between John and the Synoptic Gospels." *Journal of the Evangelical Theological Society* 41, no. 2 (June 1998).

Groothuis, Douglas. "What Jesus Thought About Women: His Regard for Them Was Unusual for His Time—Even Scandalous." *Priscilla Papers* 16, no. 3 (summer 2002).

Kent, Homer A., Jr. "How We Got Our New Testament." *Grace Journal* 8, no. 2 (spring 1967).

Köstenberger, Andreas J. "The Destruction of the Second Temple and the Composition of the Fourth Gospel." *Trinity Journal* 26, no. 2 (fall 2005).

Lane, William L. "Redaktionsgeschichte and the De-Historicizing of the New Testament Gospel." *Journal of the Evangelical Theological Society* 11, no. 1 (winter 1968).

Martinez, G. Ted. "The Purpose of John's Gospel: Part One." *Michigan Theological Journal* 3, no. 1 (spring 1992).

May, Grace. "Who's Who? New Testament Female Ministry Role Models." *Priscilla Papers* 7, no. 3 (summer 1993).

Moeller, Henry R. "Wisdom Motifs and John's Gospel." *Journal of the Evangelical Theological Society* 6, no. 3 (summer 1963).

Newman, Robert C. "The Council of Jamnia and the Old Testament Canon." *Interdisciplinary Biblical Research Institute Research Report* 13 (1983).

Nixon, John Ashley. "Who Wrote the Fourth Gospel? The Authorship and Occasion of the Fourth Gospel According to Patristic Evidence from the First Three Centuries." *Faith and Mission* 20, no. 3 (summer 2003).

Richards, E. Randolph. "An Honor/Shame Argument for Two Temple Clearings." *Trinity Journal* 29, no. 1 (spring 2008).

Tenny, Merrill C. "The Footnotes of John's Gospel." *Bibliotheca Sacra* 117, no. 468 (October 1960).

Yarbrough, Robert W. "The Date Of Papias: A Reassessment." *Journal of the Evangelical Theological Society* 26, no. 2 (June 1983).

ABOUT THE AUTHOR

*F*or many years Michael Card has struggled to listen to the Scripture at the level of the imagination. The result has been thirty-three albums and twenty-five books, all examining a different element of the Bible, from the life of the apostle Peter to slavery in the New Testament to Christ-centered creativity.

He has a master's degree in biblical studies from Western Kentucky University as well as honorary PhDs in music (Whitfield Seminary) and Christian education (Philadelphia Biblical University).

He lives with his wife, Susan, and their four children in Franklin, Tennessee, where together they pursue racial reconciliation and neighborhood renewal.

www.michaelcard.com

ABOUT THE BIBLICAL IMAGINATION SERIES

The Biblical Imagination Series is made up of four elements: commentary, music, onsite experience and community discussion. The series overviews the Gospels by means of a commentary on each of the four books, a collection of songs and a video teaching series from Israel as well as a touring conference series. For more information go to the Facebook page for "Biblical Imagination with Michael Card" or visit www.biblicalimagination.com.

Matthew: The Gospel of Identity
Mark: The Gospel of Passion
Luke: The Gospel of Amazement
John: The Gospel of Wisdom

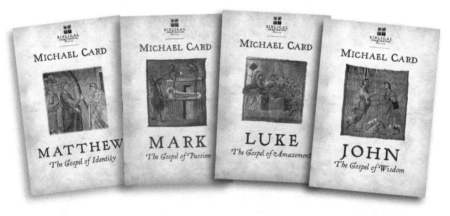

Matthew:	*Mark:*	*Luke:*	*John:*
The Gospel of Identity	The Gospel of Passion	The Gospel of	The Gospel of Wisdom
269 pages, paperback	208 pages, paperback	Amazement	240 pages, paperback
978-0-8308-3812-7	978-0-8308-3813-4	272 pages, paperback	978-0-8308-4413-5
		978-0-8308-3835-6	

ALSO AVAILABLE FROM INTERVARSITY PRESS

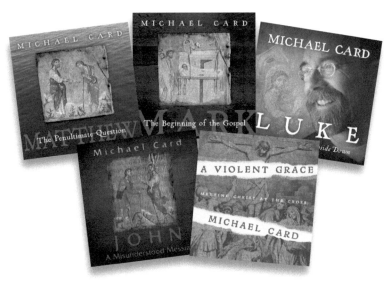

Matthew: The Penultimate Question	Mark: The Beginning of the Gospel	Luke: A World Turned Upside Down	John: A Misunderstood Messiah	A Violent Grace: Meeting Christ at the Cross
music CD	music CD	music CD	music CD	music CD
978-0-8308-3803-5	978-0-8308-3802-8	978-0-8308-3801-1	978-0-8308-3804-2	978-0-8308-3771-1

Scribbling in the Sand: Christ and Creativity	A Fragile Stone: The Emotional Life of Simon Peter	A Better Freedom: Finding Life as Slaves of Christ	A Violent Grace: Meeting Christ at the Cross
168 pages, paperback	192 pages, paperback	168 pages, paperback	182 pages, paperback
978-0-8308-3254-5	978-0-8308-3445-7	978-0-8308-3714-4	978-0-8308-3772-4